BY TIM & AMI LOPER

The Mission: Boy to Man
Published 2010
by Biblical Standards Publications
Maggie Valley, NC

in coordination with
Dream Builders, LLC
1026 W. Woodman Dr.
Tempe, AZ 85283
miracle-books@cox.net
http://members.cox.net/miracle-books/

Manufactured in the United States.
CPSIA Compliance Information: Batch # 1210.
For further information contact
RJ Communications, NY NY,
800-621-2556.

ISBN: 978-0-9678798-3-3

TABLE OF CONTENTS:

Dad and Mom,

Not only is your son embarking on a mission, you are as well. Your mission is to prepare your son for his mission to become a True Man. Your mission of godly parenthood is coming to the critical junction of puberty. We are honored that, at this time, you have chosen this book to help you undergird your strength as a parent.

Here are some helps to keep in mind as you prepare for your mission:

- Before reading this with your son, read through it yourself, preferably with your spouse.
- This book was intended for fathers to read **with** their sons. Please do not just hand this book over to your son. He needs someone to walk this road with him. If you are a single mom, you may want to find a godly man to read this with your son.
- We have purposely divided this book into two distinct sections: *The Mission I* and *The Mission II*, recognizing that a younger son, who may be ready for the first section, is likely not ready for *The Mission II*, which deals with deeper moral issues. We know that some topics in *The Mission II* may be difficult to discuss, but it is vital to discuss them openly and honestly and with a loving parent.
- Ask God to show you when to read each section of *The Mission: Boy to Man*. Only you can decide when the time is right for the son you are training.
- After reading *The Mission I* with your son around age 9, it would be wise to keep the book in your possession. As a Dad, you are endeavoring to keep your son's mind pure by not placing unnecessary information in his thoughts. Read *The Mission II* when you feel it is appropriate, probably around age 13-15. After reading *The Mission II* with your son, consider giving him the book as a handbook with Scriptural references and support for living a godly life.
- Some fathers have found taking their son out of the or-

dinary circumstances of life for a weekend enables them to open up more fully and ask the questions they otherwise might not ask.

• Proceed with caution. Be careful not to embarrass, interrupt or rush as you read through this book together. Keep your son's temperament in mind. If he needs sensitivity, give it. If he needs more time than you expected, give it. The sections of this book do not need to be read all at once. This is an opportunity to build an even stronger relationship with your son.

• Mothers, keep in mind the tremendous influence you have on the mindset of manhood that is established in your home. Allow your son to be chivalrous; don't overprotect him, but let him grow into a protector and guardian of you and his sisters. This is an essential element in helping your son develop into a man you will be proud of. For a mother who may be going through this process alone, please know that our prayers are with you. We know God will be faithful to help you step into this role.

We personally thank you for your devotion to your son and family. Parents who fulfill their calling to train their children are beautiful demonstrations of the love of our heavenly Father.

To the Glory of God,
Tim & Ami Loper

THE MISSION I

A MANUAL FOR YOUR GREAT ADVENTURES

THE MISSION I

A MANUAL FOR YOUR GREAT ADVENTURES

You are about to embark on a great mission—one filled with excitement and opportunity! Parts of this mission will be unexciting, but parts will be thrilling or even dangerous. This will be your greatest mission so far, but it will not be your last. There will be many adventures, plans of attack, and new tactics you must learn along the way.

Here are some definitions that will help you understand the terminology in this manual:

MISSION: YOUR PRIMARY GOAL.

ADVENTURES: HILLS TO CLIMB AND CONQUER.

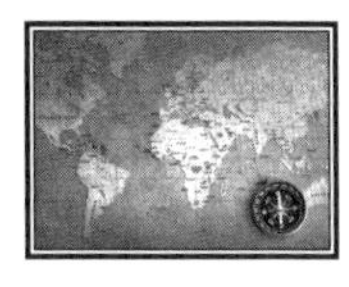

PLAN OF ATTACK: PRACTICAL ACTIONS TO ADVANCE THE MISSION.

TACTICAL REASONING: WISDOM BEHIND YOUR PLAN OF ATTACK.

COURSE SELECTION: CHOOSE YOUR PATH.

Your tour of duty for accomplishing this mission will last a long time—years, in fact. Your mission will begin at a time you cannot predict and have twists and turns that may surprise you. Though you cannot control when your mission begins, when it will end, or how fast it will go, you can control how well you respond to it and even some of its outcomes. You will not be alone on this mission. God's Word and your parents will be available to counsel and guide you. You can consider them your compass and field guides.

What is a Boy?
A promise of the future.
Energy bound up in a body.
An adventure looking for a place to happen.

What is a man?
One who protects the weak and defenseless.
One who gives of his life for those he has responsibility.
An adventure looking for a place to happen.

-Ami Loper

YOUR MISSION: BECOME A TRUE MAN

"And the boy Samuel continued to grow in stature and in favor with the Lord and with men." 1 Samuel 2:26

The mission you are on is to become a True Man. It is a noble mission, one that every boy has the choice of accepting. Not all boys accept it. It may seem strange to think that not all men become True Men, but that is a truth you will come to recognize as you grow. All boys will physically grow into men, but that is not the complete mission. This mission goes further; it requires becoming a True Man, a godly man.

BUT WHAT IS A TRUE MAN?

There are many ideas of what a man should be. Some people believe men should be tough and rough, not worrying about their own feelings or the feelings of others. Others portray men as weak and helpless, silly characters who can be made fun of.

But what does God say a man should be? When God created man, He chose to make him in His own image. "Then God said, 'Let us make man in our image, in our likeness...'" (Genesis 1:26). This means that men may reflect God's character traits. It means that God gave humans the ability to create, the right to take dominion, and the desire for relationship with Him and others.

God created the world from nothing. Man creates from what God put in the world. As a boy you create everything from mud pies and sand castles to forts and tree houses. As you become a True Man, you will create many new and awesome things. True Men create things like bridges and buildings, businesses and churches, families and homes. God gave us the potential, desire and responsibility to create. Our training to become that creative force is part of our mission.

God gave dominion of this world to us. To exercise dominion is to care for and manage what God has given you. Throughout this mission, you will have the opportunity to step up to new levels of dominion. Start by taking care of your toys and chores around the house. Then expand your dominion by learning to protect your younger siblings (especially sisters), friends, and, eventually, your mom and family. Ultimately you will exercise dominion in your job, in government, and over the environment. You will also be responsible to provide for and protect your own wife and children.

"The Lord God took the man and put him in the Garden of Eden to work it and take care of it." Genesis 2:15

God also created man to have a relationship with Him. Adam's first relationship was with God—God came and walked with Adam in the garden. Although Adam had to leave the Garden of Eden after his rebellion, God's desire for relationship with man didn't end. It continues to be our most important purpose. We are to have a close, growing, and never-ending relationship with God, like that of a father and son. When we live in that type of relationship, we will bring glory to God in all our ways.

"How great is the love the Father has lavished on us, that we should be called children of God! And that is what we are!" 1 John 3:1

Ephesians 5:1 tells us to "be imitators of God." Because we are called to be His imitators, it is important to know how God describes Himself. The entirety of God's Word is God's invitation to us to learn Who He is.

HOW DOES GOD DESCRIBE HIMSELF?

"And (God) passed in front of Moses, proclaiming, 'The Lord, the Lord, the compassionate and gracious God, slow to anger, abounding in love and faithfulness.'" Exodus 34:6

"Dear friends, let us love one another, for love comes from God. Everyone who loves has been born of God and knows God. Whoever does not love does not know God, because God is love." 1 John 4:7-8

"Who is this King of glory? The Lord strong and mighty, the Lord mighty in battle." Psalm 24:8

From the Bible we learn that men should be kind, giving, loving, strong, compassionate, faithful, and creative, just like God. "Put on the new self, created to be like God in true righteousness and holiness" (Ephesians 4:24). Growing into the person God designed you to be will move you toward becoming a True Man.

God doesn't want you to be aggressive or passive. An aggressive person is selfish, demanding, forceful, and rude. A passive person is afraid to stand up for what's right. God wants you to be assertive—ready to do the right thing and confident that God has given you the power to handle any situation. He wants you to be a giver, not a taker—not controlling, but protecting.

THE PERFECT MAN

It is impossible to become a True Man, a godly man! That is, if you try to do so alone. It is only through the help of The Perfect Man, Jesus Christ, that any of us is able to become a True

Man. If you have already asked Jesus into your heart, you have all you need inside you. "And God is able to make all grace abound to you, so that in all things at all times, having all that you need, you will abound in every good work" (2 Corinthians 9:8). It is as though a seed were planted inside you. It may not look like much now, but as you care for and water it by developing your relationship with Jesus, that seed will grow into a great and mighty tree.

As you continue to grow strong in the Lord, this tree will grow so strong that it will produce fruit for those around you to eat. The fruit of the Spirit will grow in you and the Lord will use your fruit to bless those around you!

If you have never asked Jesus into your heart, now would be the perfect time. You need Him if you want to develop into a man of wisdom and strength. Right now, pray to Him and say,

"Lord Jesus, I know that You alone are The Perfect Man and that I am not perfect, but I want to be a True Man. I know I cannot be one without You in my life so I ask You to come into my heart and life right now and plant Your seeds. I will do my best to water them and care for them by making You most important in my life. I ask You to forgive all my sins and make me sin-free in Your eyes. Thank You, Jesus for dying for me so that I can be forgiven and be Your son forever."

YOUR FIRST ADVENTURE

In the next chapter we will discuss your first adventure on this mission to become a True Man—the adventure of puberty. During puberty, the boy you look like now will develop into the body of the man God designed you to be. All boys will walk the road of puberty and develop manly bodies, but each boy must determine if he will make the choices that lead him to become a True Man. Just because a person looks like a man on the outside, doesn't mean he is one on the inside. Each boy becomes a fully developed human being without much effort; it is inevitable. You will grow and your body will change. Puberty is when each boy must decide whether or not to become a man on the inside. This is the first and biggest course selection you must make.

Your body will go through physical changes and you can't alter the outcome of those changes. However, you also will undergo changes on the inside. It is up to you to decide what kind of man you are going to be when the process is done. That decision isn't one you should choose to make at the end of this journey. A different path is required for becoming a True Man. Decide now which path to take. If you start off in the wrong direction and reach the end of the trail, it will be difficult to complete your mission.

Only you can decide what kind of a man you will be. No one else can decide for you. You were created to be the hero in your story. You are a world shaper, well equipped to make a difference and fulfill all that God has chosen you for. Study Who God is and decide to become like Him. Choose to make His character traits your character traits.

YOUR MISSION'S OBJECTIVE: Become a True Man.

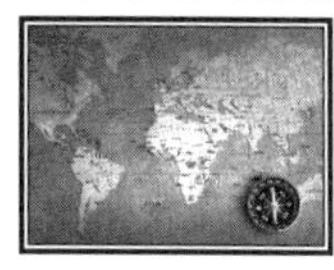

PLAN OF ATTACK: Study the character traits of God and make them yours.

TACTICAL REASONING: When it comes to your definition of what a True Man is, decide now whose voice you will listen to: God's or the world's.

COURSE SELECTION: Be a boy in a man's body or become a True Man.

YOUR FIRST ADVENTURE WITHIN THIS MISSION: Puberty

ADVENTURE #1: PUBERTY

Becoming a man physically takes time. These changes will not happen overnight, but slowly and surely, you will change. Just as a toddler no longer looks like a baby and a young boy no longer looks like a toddler, you will soon morph into a man.

Some boys will begin to change before their friends do, but all will change. There is a gland called the pituitary gland located in your brain that schedules all these physical changes for your body. The timing for each change cannot be altered. God designed this gland, so you can trust that He is in control of your changes. The pituitary gland will tell your body when to change, how much to change, and how fast to change. For most boys this begins very slowly around the age of 11 or 12, though it is perfectly normal to start as early as 9 or as late as 14. You may feel uncomfortable or awkward if you are the first to start growing or the last. Wherever you are in relation to the boys around you, trust that all your changes will happen at the right time for you.

Some changes will be more dramatic or faster than others. You will experience increased perspiration, hair and skin changes, rapid growth, muscle development, and changes in your voice.

This is an excellent time to imitate Christ and be sensitive to the feelings of those around you. No matter how they act, many boys are self-conscious and uncomfortable about their changes. Being aware of how others feel and choosing to be kind are part of being a True Man.

CHANGES REQUIRING CLEANLINESS

All changes bring new responsibilities, but you can handle them! In this adventure, the most noticeable changes will require you to adjust how you keep your body clean. For example, you will begin to have body odor. When you get hot or have been exercising, your perspiration (sweat) will begin to have a strong odor, especially to those around you. Perhaps you've noticed that your father stinks of sweat after mowing the grass or working out. The same thing will happen to you soon. You will need to take personal responsibility by showering daily (or more often) and wearing deodorant. When showering, wash well with soap all over. Just rinsing with water will not remove the body odor. Typically no one can smell himself, so don't be alarmed or upset if your mom or dad is the first to notice that it's time for you to wear deodorant. This generally is the way it happens. Your parents are your partners on this mission and want you not to offend others by smelling bad. This is a choice for the inside man to make. Good hygiene habits are a sign of love and consideration to others.

Another change is smelly feet. Perspiration can build up in closed shoes and soak into socks, causing odors to multiply. Again, responsibility is called for. Daily bathing will help, but since odor builds up through the day, it may be necessary for you to wash your feet in the evening. Make sure you wear socks with your shoes and let your shoes air out each night by storing them open and without socks stuffed inside. There are some foot sprays or powders that can help tremendously. If people are passing out when you remove your shoes in the living room, learn to take them off somewhere else and then wash your feet. Then ask your mom or dad if they can purchase foot odor products for you.

There will also be changes to your skin. Your skin will begin to produce more oil, which may clog your pores and cause pimples (often called zits). Washing your face twice a day with soap and water will help reduce pimples but be cautious about washing more than that. Over-washing can dry out your face, causing your skin to overreact and produce even more oils, creating more skin problems. Special soaps for the face may help get rid of pimples. Ask your mom or dad to help you pick one out. Then try it for a few weeks. When you start a new skin-care treatment, it often gets worse before it gets better, as the cleanser first has to unclog all those pores before you see improvement.

The extra oils in your skin may cause your hair to look dirty and greasy. You may have been able to go a couple days without a shower, but not any more. You will need to shower daily and you may even have to wash your hair twice during each shower to keep it looking clean.

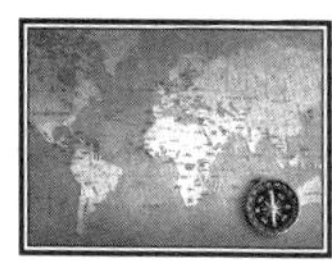

PLAN OF ATTACK: Stay clean. Soap, hot water and deodorant are your friends.

TACTICAL REASONING: A True Man takes care of what may be offensive to others. He is considerate to those around him and willing to take responsibility for himself.

"...be ready to do whatever is good, to slander no one, to be peaceable and considerate, and to show true humility toward all men." Titus 3:1-2

HAIR GROWTH

This next area of change is generally considered more exciting than body odor and pimples! You will begin to grow hair in new places. Starting from the floor and moving upward toward your face, you will notice thicker, coarser hair will begin to grow on your legs. Hair will grow around your private area, beginning with just a few hairs until eventually you have some on your lower abdomen. Hair also will grow on your chest. It will begin with a few hairs sprouting in the center of your chest and continue to spread. You'll also have some growing around your nipples. Some boys will have lots of hair while others may never acquire more than a few. This is normal and is determined by your family genetics. Contrary to what my grandfather told me, eating spinach is not going to put hair on your chest! Your underarms will also get in the act and become hairy. Girls will grow hair on their underarms as well and will have to shave them – what a pain that must be! Go True Men!

Probably the most anticipated place to grow new hair is your face. These normally are referred to as whiskers. Like all hair growth, this will begin slowly. The fine, unnoticeable hairs on your upper lip will begin to grow darker, longer, and thicker. You will notice new hairs on your cheeks by your ears. These are sideburns. Your lower lip will join in and finally whiskers will emerge on your chin.

In the beginning, all this hair growth on your face will be sparse and will look pretty scraggly. Eventually the whiskers will grow closer together. From the beginning you'll probably be wondering when you can shave. Ask your Dad! He will know when it's the right time and teach you all the tricks to do a good job. You may nick yourself a few times as you learn, but that is not a big deal; it happens to all of us.

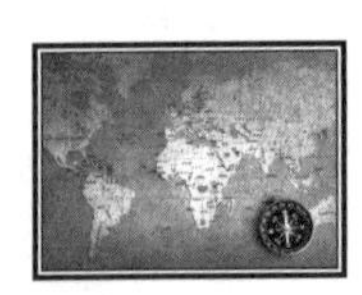

PLAN OF ATTACK: Learn to shave facial hair.

TACTICAL REASONING: A True Man learns from those who have gone before him.

"Listen, my sons, to a father's instruction; pay attention and gain understanding." Proverbs 4:1

GROWTH

You will grow more than hair on your journey through puberty. You will grow from head to toe. There will be times when you grow in height slowly and steadily. You may also experience rapid growth. These are called growth spurts. Sometimes growth spurts are accompanied by growing pains. Growing pains are aches and pains in your larger muscles—usually in your thighs or calves. There is nothing wrong with you when this happens; it simply means you are getting ready to grow taller. Pain generally occurs in the late part of the day and at night, but is gone by morning.

You may notice that the girls your age are growing taller before you. Girls usually begin their growth spurts earlier than boys. But don't worry; they also stop growing earlier than boys. Girls stop growing around age 16 while boys don't stop until their early twenties! If you haven't started really growing yet, don't worry. Talk to your dad and ask him when he started his growth spurts. If you are wondering how tall you will be, know that height is hereditary. Look at how tall the men in your family are—your father, uncles, and grandfathers.

Indeed, you will be growing all over. As your body, arms, and legs grow, your hands and feet will grow. There may be times when an almost brand new pair of shoes suddenly does not fit or you need to buy pants a bit long so that they last longer.

Not only will there be times when your clothes don't fit, there may be times when you don't feel like you fit in your own body! You may feel clumsy and awkward as you quickly acquire height and length in your limbs. This is common and nothing to worry about. Keep exercising and being active; it will help you adjust to your growing body. You'll get used to the new you before you know it and soon feel at home in your own body.

Another area where men and boys differ is that men have larger muscles and broader shoulders. Though no one develops big muscles automatically, natural hormones cause muscle growth and change the proportions of your body. All men differ in this regard as well; some men are genetically designed by God to be tall and slender while others are naturally large and look like football players. It is not important to have the largest muscles or to be the fastest boy in school. It is important to get plenty of physical exercise and develop your strength and physical health. Everyone differs in athletic ability, just as they do in academic ability. It is key to attempt new things and be the best you can be at whatever you are involved in.

Whether you have worked out to be on the wrestling team or not, men are naturally stronger than most women. For this reason it is important that you learn to be gentle with those who are smaller or weaker than you. This can be difficult; many young men are largely unaware of their newfound strength. I learned this when I accidentally cracked my grandmother's rib one day while hugging her goodbye! Take extra care with sisters, younger brothers, mom, grandmas, and the elderly. Your role is to protect them, not to toss them around like sacks of potatoes!

Here is a place to exercise your True Man, your character, and find ways to serve those around you with your new strength! Carry groceries for mom, pull in your neighbor's trash barrels, or weed the yard of the elderly couple down the street. These are all great ways to give God the glory for the strength He has given you.

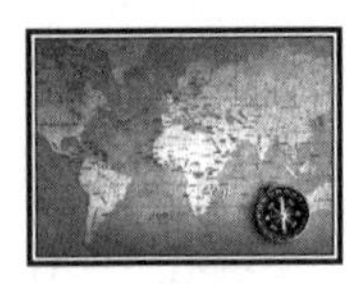

PLAN OF ATTACK: Master your strength.

TACTICAL REASONING: Be strong, but realize that strength brings responsibility. A True Man never picks on someone who is smaller or weaker than he is. He knows when to be strong and when to be gentle. He recognizes that his strength is given to him so that he is better equipped to serve those around him.

"Be…temperate, self-controlled, respectable…, not violent but gentle, not quarrelsome." 1 Timothy 3:2-3

YOUR VOICE

During puberty your voice will begin to change. It will get deeper and sound manlier. This happens because the parts in your throat that produce sound are growing, just like the rest of you. Your vocal cords are getting thicker and longer and your voice box, or larynx, is growing larger. This will produce a lump on the front of your neck often called an "Adam's apple."

The transition from a higher boy's voice to a deeper man's voice generally is not a smooth one. The process is gradual and there will be times when your voice suddenly transitions from low to high or high to low. This happens frequently to all boys and is called having your voice "crack." Having your voice crack can feel embarrassing, but it's important to remember that you are in transition and this eventually will stop as your vocal cords strengthen. Some boys get nervous when they speak and tighten the muscles in their throats. This can make their voices crack even more. Relaxing can go a long way toward keeping your voice steady.

Don't take this change too seriously! You can laugh at yourself when your voice cracks and others may laugh right along with you. Staying light-hearted about the changes you are going through will make them easier.

PLAN OF ATTACK: Have fun in the midst of change.

TACTICAL REASONING: You can choose to be embarrassed about your changing voice or decide that change is a good thing and welcome it!

"Don't let anyone look down on you because you are young." 1 Timothy 4:12

DISCRETION

You are learning many new and interesting things about your body. It may be tempting to use this information in the wrong way. One way to do this is to speak unkindly about others' changes. A wise young man doesn't offend with his mouth, but masters his tongue. The apostle James compares the tongue to the rudder of a ship. How you use your tongue will influence your life and impact others. You can choose to build up or to tear down. The choice is yours. You have a profound impact on those you criticize or encourage. You must learn when and how to speak. You must be careful to express God's view to those around you.

For this reason you should avoid speaking about a person's weight, height, or physical characteristics. Even comments you may consider to be a positive evaluation of a person need to be said carefully and thoughtfully. I describe myself as a tall, lean person; others may call me skinny. To me "skinny" isn't a compliment. This is true for comments directed toward guys and girls. We should verbally compliment those we love, to bless and encourage them, but those compliments should not be focused on a specific physical attribute. God looks at the heart; we would do well to direct our compliments toward the heart as well. We should train ourselves to focus on a person's kindness, generosity, patience, grace and wisdom.

Some people use words that are offensive and rude. These generally are referred to as curse words or swear words. Sometimes young men use offensive language because they hear others using it. Perhaps you have been tempted to swear to fit in or when you are angry. Swearing is never necessary to communicate your feelings. You may think that because some adults swear, it is a sign of adulthood. Swearing is not an indication of maturity. A mature man finds ways to express himself without losing control of his tongue. Swearing doesn't glorify God and is not the behavior of a True Man. It proves a young man is immature and reveals a lack of self-control in older men.

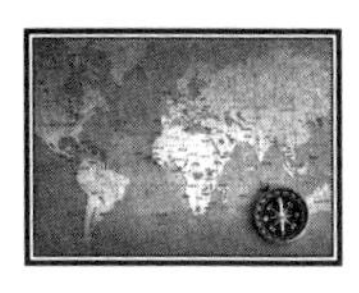

PLAN OF ATTACK: Master your tongue. Know what to say and when to say it.

TACTICAL REASONING: A True Man knows how to use discretion. A man has the power to build up or tear down with his words. A True Man builds up those around him and keeps his speech pure.

"Therefore encourage one another and build each other up, just as in fact you are doing." 1 Thessalonians 5:11

"Nor should there be obscenity, foolish talk or coarse joking, which are out of place, but rather thanksgiving." Ephesians 5:4

"Or take ships as an example. Although they are so large and are driven by strong winds, they are steered by a very small rudder wherever the pilot wants to go. Likewise the tongue is a small part of the body, but it makes great boasts. Consider what a great forest is set on fire by a small spark." James 3:4-5

MANNERS

Every young man needs to learn a few manners. Things that were acceptable when you were a little boy may not be acceptable now. When we are newborn babies our minds and bodies are without discipline. Slowly we learn how to do things. We learn everything from clapping to running, from talking to using the bathroom. Along the way we also learn when to clap, when to run, and when to excuse ourselves to the bathroom. Rules that dictate when activities are appropriate, or inappropriate, are called "manners." There are many things we can do, but they are not always appropriate, depending on where we are or whom we are with. Our Biblical goal is to be considerate of others—it is an effective way to show love to those around us.

A specific example of manners and a valuable expression of love is control of bodily noises, like burping. When you let out a long, loud burp you may earn the admiration of your friends, but doing so in front of your mom or sister will get you banished to your room. There is a time for having fun with burps, but it isn't just any time! Our intent should be to love those around us and accept that some bodily noises may not be appropriate in some contexts. For instance, when ladies are around, avoid burping and excuse yourself when that burp slips out when you weren't expecting it!

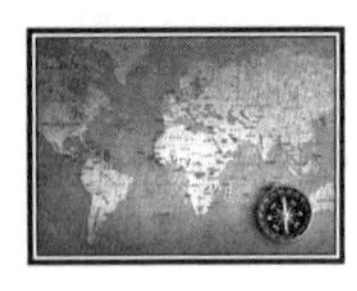

PLAN OF ATTACK: Learn what behaviors are inappropriate in certain settings.

TACTICAL REASONING: A True Man is considerate. He does his best to not offend those around him and apologizes when he does so accidentally.

"But the wisdom that comes from heaven is first of all pure; then peace-loving, considerate, submissive, full of mercy and good fruit, impartial and sincere." James 3:17

HORMONES

The pituitary gland that is causing all these changes in your body does so by sending out chemicals called "hormones." While these hormones cause all the wonderful and exciting changes to your body, they also have side effects.

Hormones can make your chest sore and swollen around your nipples. Some boys think their hormones have messed up and that they are developing breasts. However, this is common and temporary. The soreness and swelling will go away.

Another effect is that you may feel moody from time to time. There may be times when you have a sudden urge to get angry or cry or be sullen and anti-social. While there is nothing wrong with emotions in and of themselves, each person must choose to behave well, to control his responses no matter how he is feeling. Hormones cannot be used as an excuse for bad behavior. Though hormones are a fact of life, how you respond to them is entirely your decision. Your feelings will not always be accurate. That is where trusting comes in. Trusting means you act based on God's Word and what you've been taught, not on your feelings. Trust that God will help you through life's challenges and that your parents love and care for you. Learning to trust what you know, instead of what you may be feeling, will help you to remain steady and avoid conflict.

PLAN OF ATTACK: Master your emotions.

TACTICAL REASONING: A True Man controls his temper and doesn't allow his temper to control him.

"My dear brothers, take note of this: Everyone should be quick to listen, slow to speak and slow to become angry, for man's anger does not bring about the righteous life that God desires." James 1:19-20

"A fool gives full vent to his anger, but a wise man keeps himself under control." Proverbs 29:11

HUNGER AND ENERGY

With all this growth going on, it is important that you take care of your body. You likely will notice that you are hungrier than usual—sometimes a lot hungrier! It's important that you give your body the food it needs: healthy foods that will help your body grow stronger. A growing body needs plenty of food to develop into the body of an adult man. While you are growing, your body is using amazing amounts of energy. Fuel your body with the good food it needs. Keep in mind that although junk food tastes good and will give you a full feeling, it rarely has the nutrients your body needs. Make sure you eat lots of protein (meats, eggs, nuts, beans, and dairy products, for example) and fruits and vegetables every day.

Amid all this growth and development, at times you may feel tired. When you are feeling tired, you still will need to maintain good habits. A good night's sleep and eating well can help your body kick the over-tired feeling; but if it persists, you still need to choose to keep up with your responsibilities at home and school. If you give in to fatigue or choose to eat poorly and avoid exercise, you will develop unhealthy lifetime habits that are very hard to break.

Other times you will have an almost overwhelming abundance of energy. You will need to find a positive way to use this energy. Wrestle with your dad or older brother, get involved in a sport, lift weights, go for a run, ride a bike, or go for a swim. Spend some of that energy in a beneficial way and remember that you can't be rough with just anyone. Exercise will help you to maintain your self-control.

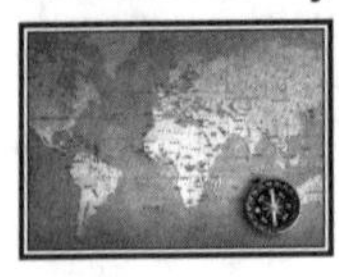

PLAN OF ATTACK: Eat right and exercise.

TACTICAL REASONING: A True Man takes care of his body and has self-control over his impulses.

"Therefore, prepare your minds for action; be self-controlled."
1 Peter 1:13

GOING FORWARD

Right now you are bridging two worlds. It is natural to one day have the attitude of a man and the next day to have the attitude of a boy. This will happen less and less as you grow and yield to the changes. Gradually you will have fewer days of acting childish and more days of taking responsibility for yourself and caring for others.

"Childishness" is doing immature things that are not appropriate for the man you are becoming. You must choose to leave behind what is "childish." On the other hand, doing things that you know are wrong or sinful is called "foolishness." Your parents have laid a solid foundation for you to know right from wrong. They are there to help you make right choices. You must choose to do what is right and reject "foolishness." Listen to your parents' wisdom to become a wise man.

It is by making good daily decisions that you become a True Man. This does not happen overnight or on your eighteenth birthday. You must choose daily to stay on the path to become a True Man.

COURSE SELECTION: Your physical changes are uncontrollable, but your responses to them are controllable. How do you choose to respond?

ADVENTURE #2: YOUR ABILITIES

Along with puberty, you are destined for even more adventures! One of them is discovering and developing your natural abilities. God has given abilities to each human being. These are talents or strengths that make life fun and interesting and they are avenues through which you can glorify God. It blesses God's heart to see His children use and enjoy His gifts and give Him thanks and credit for them.

There are many different types of abilities and the Lord may have blessed you with more than one! Each ability is important and valuable to you and the Kingdom of God. Each person's abilities make him unique and special and each person's uniqueness gives our world excitement and flavor and different ways of bringing glory to God. If everyone had the same abilities, life would be boring and predictable, so celebrate your abilities and the abilities of others.

"(God) has filled him with the Spirit of God, with skill, ability and knowledge in all kinds of crafts." Exodus 35:31

"To these four young men God gave knowledge and understanding of all kinds of literature and learning. And Daniel could understand visions and dreams of all kinds." Daniel 1:17

It's important to try many different activities. Until you try something diligently, you don't know if it will reveal a natural ability. Some young men are gifted in the area of sports. They may enjoy participating in team sports. Others may like the activity, but not the competition. If that describes you, you may want to try weight lifting, rock climbing, biking, swimming, jogging, skating, or kayaking. There are so many different sports and activities; you probably will find one that's right for you and helps you develop a healthy body and lifestyle. Remember, you don't have to be the best at something for it to be your special ability. Just have fun, try hard and don't worry about who is the best.

You, and other boys like you, simply may not be athletically inclined. That is just fine. You should focus on your God-given abilities, not one He gave to someone else. Nevertheless, even if you are not athletic, you should find a physical activity that you can enjoy. It will help your body to be healthy and it will give you an outlet for the excess energy experienced during puberty.

Some boys really enjoy academics. Whether they enjoy math and science or literature and writing, they recognize that God has blessed them with ability and enthusiasm for study. Some boys may like broad aspects of a subject while others prefer the specifics. For instance, some may love to study history in general while others prefer a specific ancient society, the Civil War or naval history.

Even if you aren't gifted academically, it is important to do your best at school. The things you learn at school will help you in every part of your life and can affect your other natural abilities. Be persistent. Natural abilities aren't always evident right away. Thomas Edison's teachers considered him dull and unable to learn and he went on to invent recorded sound and the light bulb! Persistence and hard work—those are characteristics of a True Man.

Many men are gifted in the arts. They may sing, paint, play an instrument, act, cook, or write poetry. The list goes on and on! Whatever your ability, you will find that art can bless your life and minister to those around you. After all, your abilities were not given to you just for you to enjoy, they are for the Kingdom of God and His glory.

Some people find their abilities in working with people. Perhaps they speak well in groups and have a talent for leadership. Maybe they know just the right words when a friend needs counsel. Their gift of getting along well with others and making others feel comfortable is just the ability God needs them to have so they can reach those around them.

Other people work well with their hands. They take things apart to figure out how they work or perhaps they like building new things. Some who enjoy working with their hands find their ability in gardening or as a mechanic working on cars or jet airplanes.

It's important to always be a "good sport," whether your abilities lie in sports, academics, the arts, working with people or working with your hands. This means appreciating others' abilities, not thinking them lesser or greater than your own. It means persevering. It means never participating in or encouraging name-calling. It means submitting to those in leadership (coaches, teachers, instructors, parents). It means that you don't demand to have things your way, but consider those around you. It means you always do your best, try new things, and never make excuses for your poor behavior or performances. "Do not let any unwholesome talk come out of your mouths, but only what is helpful for building others up according to their needs, that it may benefit those who listen" (Ephesians 4:29).

Specific abilities do not make you a True Man. It is how you use your abilities, the discipline you put in to using them and the way you dedicate them to God that sets you apart as a True Man.

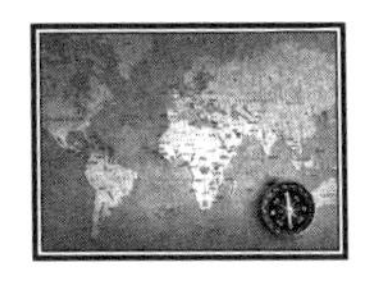

PLAN OF ATTACK: Find your natural abilities by trying different activities. Grow and develop your talents.

TACTICAL REASONING: A True Man doesn't waste what has been given to him by God. Make full use of every ability to give God glory.

COURSE SELECTION: It is important to note that all natural abilities will bring glory. Every young man must decide to whom he will bring that glory. He can choose to have the glory belong to himself by not acknowledging that God is the Source of his ability. He can bring glory to Satan by doing things with his abilities that are contrary to the Word and will of God. Or he can bring glory to God by praising Him and serving others. Choose well!

"...fan into flame the gift of God..." 2 Timothy 1:6

ADVENTURE #3: YOUR CALLING

God has placed a calling on each person who has given his heart and life to Him through His Son, Jesus. As Ephesians 1:11 says, "In him we were also chosen, having been predestined according to the plan of him who works out everything in conformity with the purpose of his will." You have a critical mission from God that only you can do. No one can fulfill your calling for you. If you don't know what your calling is yet, don't worry. God will reveal it to you when the time is right. But be assured: You have a place and purpose in this world.

There is a difference between your natural abilities, as we discussed in the last chapter, and your calling. Your natural abilities are the raw materials and your calling is what God wants to do with them. For instance, as a boy, King David had the ability to tend his flock of sheep, to worship God, and to defend the helpless sheep. Those were some of his natural abilities. His calling, that is, what God had in store for him, was to lead all of Israel—to shepherd people, to lead Israel in worshipping God, and to defend the defenseless.

One of the ways that God may reveal your calling is through your natural abilities. The talents and abilities God gives you are not random. He gives them to you for a purpose beyond just making you happy —He desires to bless others through you. Your personal adventure is to ask the Lord to reveal His calling and to have a heart that is willing to follow where He leads.

"'I have found David son of Jesse a man after my own heart; he will do everything I want him to do.'" Acts 13:22

David was a man after God's own heart because he earnestly sought out what God wanted him to do and then did God's will with all his might. This is the calling and mission of every True Man. There is no higher calling than to follow God wholeheartedly in the direction He leads you. No matter what God has called you to do, do your very best.

"And whatever you do, whether in word or deed, do it all in the name of the Lord Jesus, giving thanks to God the Father through him." Colossians 3:17

A calling is a great thing. Your calling includes being a part of God's Kingdom and His expression of His Kingdom in this world. It means living your life in a way that directs all that you do. This may not make you a preacher when you grow up, but it will include leading your family in the ways of God. You may become an honest and trusted mechanic or a businessman who gives generously to God's work. God calls each of us to use our gifts to bring glory to His name. It begins with being Christ-like in whatever you do.

"...I urge you to live a life worthy of the calling you have received." Ephesians 4:1

"Trust in the Lord with all your heart and lean not on your own understanding; in all your ways acknowledge him, and he will make your paths straight." Proverbs 3:5-6

PLAN OF ATTACK: Be aware that God has a special purpose for you. It is your calling. Listen for His leading so you can know what it is.

TACTICAL REASONING: A True Man follows God with all he has. He doesn't sit on the sidelines, but is willing and prepared to do whatever God calls him to do.

COURSE SELECTION: Choose to fulfill your calling wholeheartedly!

"Whatever you do, work at it with all your heart, as working for the Lord, not for men, since you know that you will receive an inheritance from the Lord as a reward. It is the Lord Christ you are serving." Colossians 3:23-24

MISSION REVIEW

MISSION: BECOME A TRUE MAN

COURSE SELECTION: You can choose to become a boy in a man's body or a True Man, according to God's definition of a True Man.

ADVENTURE #1: PUBERTY

Your first adventure is puberty. As you go through puberty you will need to have the following plan of attack:

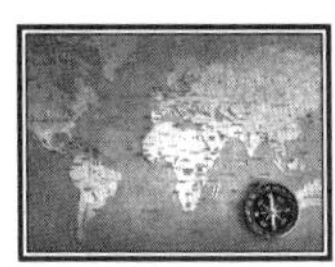

PLAN OF ATTACK:

In all the changes that you will face during puberty, purpose to:

- Stay clean to avoid offending those around you,
- Learn to shave,
- Master your strength for proper use,
- Wait out your voice changes patiently,
- Use discretion and manners,
- Master your emotions,
- Eat right and exercise.

TACTICAL REASONING: The tactical reasons behind your plans are to be a courteous, wise and responsible steward of what God has given you. (Stewardship is taking care of what has been entrusted to you.)

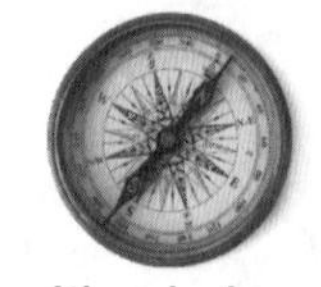

COURSE SELECTION: Do you choose to respond to the changes in your body as a godly young man? Do you choose to take on adventure with wisdom and welcome your new responsibilities?

ADVENTURE #2: YOUR ABILITIES

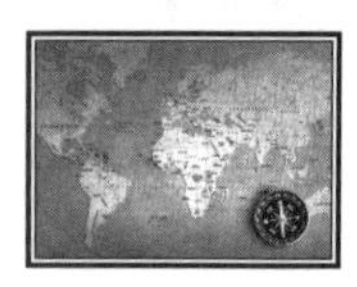

PLAN OF ATTACK: Find your natural abilities by trying different activities. Grow and develop your talents.

TACTICAL REASONING: A True Man doesn't waste what has been given to him by God. He makes full use of every ability to give God glory.

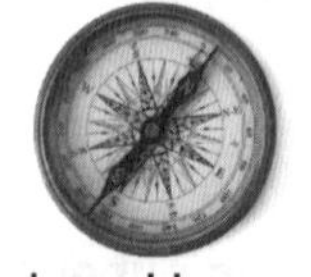

COURSE SELECTION: It is important to note that all natural abilities will bring glory. Every young man must decide to whom he will bring that glory. He can choose to have the glory belong to himself by not acknowledging that God is the Source of his ability. He can bring glory to Satan by doing things with his abilities that are contrary to the Word and will of God. Or he can bring glory to God by praising Him and serving others. Choose well!

ADVENTURE #3: YOUR CALLING

PLAN OF ATTACK: Be aware that God has a special purpose for you. It is your calling. Listen for His leading so you can know what it is.

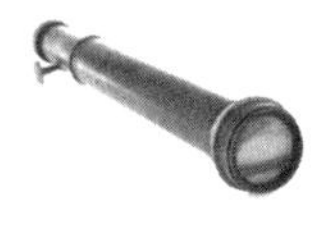

TACTICAL REASONING: A True Man follows God with all he has. He doesn't sit on the sidelines, but is willing and prepared to do whatever God calls him to do.

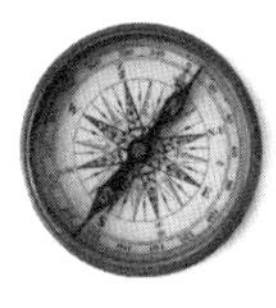

COURSE SELECTION: Choose to fulfill your calling wholeheartedly!

THE MISSION II

A MANUAL FOR YOUR GREAT WAR

THE MISSION II

A MANUAL FOR YOUR GREAT WAR

Welcome to **SECTION II** of **THE MISSION: BOY TO MAN**. Your parents have decided that it is time for you to undertake the second phase of your mission in becoming a True Man.

Keep in mind the definitions from **SECTION I**:

MISSION: YOUR PRIMARY GOAL.

ADVENTURES: HILLS TO CLIMB AND CONQUER.

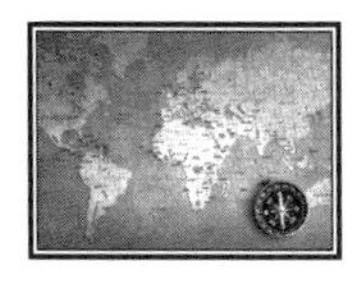

PLAN OF ATTACK: PRACTICAL ACTIONS TO ADVANCE THE MISSION.

TACTICAL REASONING: WISDOM BEHIND YOUR PLAN OF ATTACK.

COURSE SELECTION: CHOOSE YOUR PATH.

While **THE MISSION I** is about the adventure of puberty, **THE MISSION II** is about the war you will fight to successfully become a True Man. Have no doubt; the enemy is waging a war against every future man's mission. But have no fear; with God's help, you will defeat the enemy and accomplish your mission. With the help of God, your parents and this book, you will know where the grenades are likely to be thrown; you will learn to detect infiltrations and develop plans of attack; and you will learn tactical reasoning that will help you avoid becoming a casualty. You can win. You have what it takes!

“Finally, be strong in the Lord and in his mighty power. Put on the full armor of God so that you can take your stand against the devil’s schemes. For our struggle is not against flesh and blood, but against the rulers, against the authorities, against the powers of this dark world and against the spiritual forces of evil in the heavenly realms. Therefore put on the full armor of God, so that when the day of evil comes, you may be able to stand your ground, and after you have done everything, to stand. Stand firm then, with the belt of truth buckled around your waist, with the breastplate of righteousness in place, and with your feet fitted with the readiness that comes from the gospel of peace. In addition to all this, take up the shield of faith, with which you can extinguish all the flaming arrows of the evil one. Take the helmet of salvation and the sword of the Spirit, which is the word of God. And pray in the Spirit on all occasions with all kinds of prayers and requests. With this in mind, be alert and always keep on praying for all the saints.”

Ephesians 6:10-18

GET ARMED! THE BATTLE IS ON!

THE NEW YOU

In **THE MISSION I** we discussed the many changes your body will go through as you embark upon the adventure of puberty. You have undoubtedly changed and have taken on the new responsibilities that come with those changes. By now you are showering daily to keep your body clean and inoffensive to those around you. You have probably grown taller and look forward to growing even more. You're learning to master your strength and maybe even have shaved a few whiskers off your chin or upper lip. Perhaps your voice is in the process of changing. You are learning to take care of your body by eating well and getting the rest and exercise you need. Finally, you are taking care of your heart by being responsible for your emotions.

The adventure of puberty is full of fascinating transformations. As you experience them, don't forget about the other adventures it is time for you to have. Have you explored your abilities? Are you exercising them? God never wants you to bury your abilities, but to use them so that they will grow. Are you praying and listening for your calling? If you haven't heard from God yet, don't be concerned. God shows some young men their callings early, but asks others to wait until they are young adults. The important thing is to be listening. The spiritual muscles you develop by listening to God are part of the goal! As long as your ear is attentive, God will be faithful to tell you when the time is right.

Are you ready for some new adventures and changes? The second half of puberty is more intense than the first. It is more like a war than an adventure, but God created this part as well. You were created for this war, so it is nothing you cannot handle. You have been given what soldiers call your "fighting load." This means that whatever you need, you have. As Christians we know that this is true because 2 Peter 1:3-4 says, "His divine power has given us everything we need for life and godliness through our knowledge of him who called us by his own glory and goodness. Through these he has given us his very great and precious promises, so that through them you may participate in the divine nature and escape the corruption in the world caused by evil desires." Rest assured that you have every tool at your disposal through the guidance of God.

PLAN OF ATTACK: Prepare yourself for the next phase of life, remembering all you've learned thus far.

TACTICAL REASONING: Being prepared is a critical factor in any battle. Utilize the wisdom of those who have walked this road before you to make the most of your journey into adulthood and to avoid common mistakes.

COURSE SELECTION: You can choose whether to prepare for this journey. As you set out, make sure you watch for marker signs along the road and follow the Lord's direction.

A WAR? REALLY?

"Then the dragon was enraged at the woman and went off to make war against the rest of her offspring – those who obey God's commandments and hold to the testimony of Jesus."
Revelation 12:17

"For though we live in the world, we do not wage war as the world does. The weapons we fight with are not the weapons of the world. On the contrary, they have divine power to demolish strongholds. We demolish arguments and every pretension that sets itself up against the knowledge of God, and we take captive every thought to make it obedient to Christ. And we will be ready to punish every act of disobedience, once your obedience is complete."
2 Corinthians 10:3 - 6

You may be tempted to think that all this talk about war is overly dramatic or exaggerated. You've never seen a bomb go off in the mall or at the cafeteria table that leaves a bunch of guys helpless and bleeding! But I assure you that a very real war is going on in the spiritual realm and some are wounded for life by it. It is a fatal error to ignore the enemy.

The war being fought is for the purity of your heart. Your enemy, Satan, wants to sabotage your mission to become a True Man. Of course, God wants you to fulfill your mission. So who will win? It's really up to you. You must choose whose side you are going to fight on— God's or Satan's. The battlefield is your mind and the prize will be your heart.

In Genesis 4:7, God warns Cain before he is about to sin, "If you do what is right, will you not be accepted? But if you do not do what is right, sin is crouching at your door; it desires to have you, but you must master it." Essentially, God is saying that Satan wishes to have you for his very own and when you choose to go the wrong direction, he will seize upon you.

What does Satan want to do with you? If you are a child of God, Satan knows that he cannot gain your spirit, but he can make you ineffective for God. This is one of his favorite strategies. Satan is scared of you and all you can become. You can do serious damage to his kingdom if you become a True Man. But if the guilt and shame of impurity render you ineffective, Satan won't have to worry about you fulfilling God's calling and purpose. God will still love you, but He will not be able to use you as a warrior.

Though it may seem that the whole world has given up and fallen victim in this war, God has preserved for Himself a remnant that will continue to fight. This remnant will triumph and help save other wounded men. You can be part of this remnant—a survivor and a victor. God does not ask you to be a True Man and then provide no means for you to succeed. He desires to help you in this fight more than you can imagine. This war is your test, but you can win it!

"I have fought the good fight, I have finished the race, I have kept the faith." 2 Timothy 4:7

"No temptation has seized you except what is common to man. And God is faithful; he will not let you be tempted beyond what you can bear. But when you are tempted, he will also provide a way out so that you can stand up under it."
1 Corinthians 10:13

WHOSE SIDE ARE YOU ON?

Let's be clear about the battle lines. Obviously, God is on one side, fighting for you with all the powers of heaven. Jesus is on God's side, ready to remove your sins and give you righteousness. The Holy Spirit is on God's side, available to counsel and teach, faithfully speaking in your ear when the enemy throws his grenades. Also on His side are your parents and your Christian friends who want to see you succeed in becoming a True Man. If you have declared your commitment to God by accepting Jesus Christ as your Savior, then you have the power of God within you to fight these battles.

If you have not accepted God's gift of redemption, then you are trying to fight without the power of God. If that is the situation, then stop now and enlist on God's side; stop and pray, "Lord Jesus, I see that I am a sinner, that I need your forgiveness. I believe that you are the Son of God and that your sacrifice on the cross and resurrection from the dead is a gift I can accept. Thank you for the love you have shown me. Thank you for forgiving me. Please give me the Holy Spirit that I may fight the battles in my life knowing I am on your side. Amen"

Fighting on the other side is Satan, the enemy of your soul. He has his own legions calling out to you, tempting you to go on the wrong path. They want you to look too long at impurity and to allow those thoughts to remain in your mind. He may enlist some of your friends to speak his lies or lead you astray. He may find some girls who are willing to tempt you off course.

In the middle of this war are two strange characters who play the biggest parts of all. They are in constant battle with one another. As one grows stronger, the other weakens. They are both part of you! You can choose which one to strengthen by feeding one and starving the other. If you feed the one who fights for the enemy, he will overpower the one who fights for God. But if you feed the one who fights on God's side, you will defeat the enemy. These two adversaries are the "flesh" and the "spirit." Your flesh fights on the enemy's side and your spirit fights on God's side. How much you feed one or the other will tell you whether you fight on God's side or Satan's. If you choose to feed your flesh, you make him stronger and help Satan to attack you. If you choose to feed your spirit, you will win God's battles. It is that simple.

Though it is simple, it is not always easy. Your flesh will call out to be fed and it can be very persuasive. Be prepared to say no to it and yes to your spirit even when it is difficult. Oftentimes, our flesh screams out to be fed; however, our spirit may be so quiet we can barely hear it. It is only as you feed your spirit more and more that you will be able to hear it above the loud clamor of your flesh.

So how do you feed these two? You feed your flesh when you watch things that are inappropriate, give into temptation, and listen to the enemy's lies. Every time you do these things, your flesh grows stronger and bolder.

You feed your spirit every time you choose to do what is right, turn away when your flesh wants to continue looking, hide the Word of God in your heart, and speak God's Word whenever the enemy tries to speak lies. Remember, it is entirely up to you. The one you feed is the one who will become stronger.

Keep in mind that though the enemy is strong, your God is stronger. God has not created you to lose. He has given you all you need to win this war. When you fight, don't fight in fear. Fight in the knowledge that you have chosen to be on God's side and "if God is for us, who can be against us?" (Romans 8:31). Pursue God with all your heart and watch Him fight on your behalf!

"Submit yourselves, then, to God. Resist the devil, and he will flee from you. Come near to God and he will come near to you. Wash your hands, you sinners, and purify your hearts, you double-minded." James 4:7 - 8

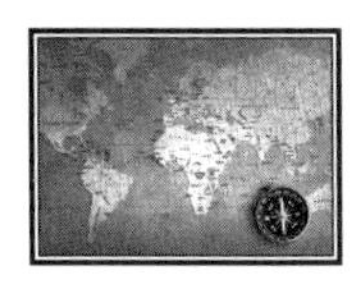

PLAN OF ATTACK: Be aware that the battles in this war are real!

TACTICAL REASONING: Be prepared to fight and have confidence that you can win. This is what you were made for.

COURSE SELECTION: Feed your spirit each day so that it will be strong in the battle with your flesh.

"The one who sows to please his sinful nature, from that nature will reap destruction; the one who sows to please the Spirit, from the Spirit will reap eternal life." Galatians 6:8

"...train yourself to be godly." 1 Timothy 4:7

A WAY OF ESCAPE

It is important to understand that to be tempted is not a sin. Even Jesus was tempted. The line of demarcation is when you choose to sin when tempted. If you give in to the enemy, you lose the battle. But every time you resist Satan, you are one battle closer to winning the war.

The enemy will chase you into an ambush and bombard you with grenades. However, he's been using the same tactics for all time, so listen to God and voices of experience. Then you can predict the ambushes and avoid them.

"And God is faithful; he will not let you be tempted beyond what you can bear. But when you are tempted, he will also provide a way out so that you can stand up under it."
1 Corinthians 10:13

Did you read that verse? You can fight this war when you know what God says about temptation. Notice how the verse says, "***when*** you are tempted..." not "if." God knows that you will be tempted and He always offers you a way out. Being tempted is generally not your fault, but you must be strong and take the way of escape God shows you to avoid sin. Your actions following the temptation are crucial: if you fail to walk away, then you have sinned.

No one but Christ is perfect. God knows you may succumb to temptation. When you fail, try not to flounder on the battlefield, where the enemy can continue to bombard you with grenades. Get up, dust yourself off, ask for forgiveness, and move forward with renewed strength and wisdom. Just because you've lost a battle doesn't mean you've lost the war! Always get back up. Confess your sin to God and ask His forgiveness. He is ready and willing to forgive, lift you onto your feet, and help you move on.

If you continue to fall, make sure your plan for avoiding grenades is effective. Evaluate your strategies and assess your battle plan. Go to your dad and God (your Base of Operations) and prepare for the next attack. Develop a battle plan checklist. Are you guarding your eyes and ears? Are you avoiding tempting situations? Do you have fellow soldiers who are watching your back? Have you hidden the Word of God in your heart? Regularly ask yourself these questions. Do you have a battle plan?

In every battle plan there needs to be a "way of escape" so you can avoid an injury. What is your way of escape? What are you going to do so you don't fall into sin? Keep in mind that the enemy can attack at any time, when you least expect it, and in places where you have failed before. He knows your weak points and will launch a surprise raid against your mind and heart. Your job is to unravel his plan by having one of your own. Don't let him disrupt communication with your Base of Operations. Don't let him make you unwilling to fight. Don't let his harassing fire lower your morale and make you surrender. Fight the good fight! Repel his assault by the power of God that lives inside you. Have a plan to mount a counterattack.

Boxes like the one to the right contain ideas other young men and adult men have used to avoid grenades and injuries. Find something that works for you! Find your own way of escape!

"There is no temptation that is uncommon to man. God will send you a way of escape, but you've got to be willing to take the escape."
~ DR

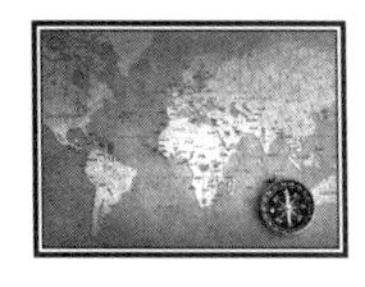

PLAN OF ATTACK: Have a plan in place, a ready response to use against the enemy's schemes.

TACTICAL REASONING: The enemy will hit you when you're down and attack when you are at your weakest. If you fall, he will be quick to condemn you to keep you down. Have hope. God will forgive you and give you a second chance.

COURSE SELECTION: God will give you a way of escape and help you gain wisdom so that you do not fall again. Will you take the Way of Escape?

"To you, O Lord, I lift up my soul; in you I trust, O my God. Do not let me be put to shame, nor let my enemies triumph over me. No one whose hope is in you will ever be put to shame." Psalm 25:1-3

"We must strive, run, struggle to overcome it, knowing that God will NEVER tempt us beyond what we are able." ~ PC

BATTLE GROUND: PHYSICAL DEVELOPMENT

There are two changes that we did not discuss in **THE MISSION I**. The first concerns your physical development. The second concerns how you process the information around you. You will begin to think differently about what you see and experience. This awakening is normal and natural, yet these changes initiate a battle for control of your mind and heart. In this battle, you will face course selections that have moral consequences. The enemy takes advantage of these changes, launching new attempts to foil your main mission: Becoming a True Man.

The changes are not from the enemy, he does not cause them to happen; he only tries to twist them and make them useful to his goal. Your body is wonderful, ordained and created by God. Nevertheless, you must make moral choices to keep your mission on the right track. Now that you have grown in moral maturity, you can make the right choices. Now is the time to become what God has called you to be: a man of God.

The first noticeable change is in your physical development. Like your entire body, your private area will begin to change and develop. If the Lord wills it, one day you will marry and you and your wife may want to have children. In order for this to happen, your body will need to develop.

During puberty, which begins for boys around the age of 9 to 14, you may have noticed that your testicles and penis began to grow larger. Your testicles moved lower and one testicle may be lower than the other; this is normal. The testicles are part of the male anatomy that God created to produce and store the seed (sperm). Sperm is the portion God has given to men that is required, along with the portion from his wife (the egg), to create a baby.

As you develop, there may be times when your penis reacts without reason or warning and becomes unexpectedly stiff and straight. This is called an erection. You may have experienced this already. This may happen because you're nervous or excited, because of something you have seen, or just because your bladder is too full or your clothes are too tight. Although an erection can be surprising, it is a normal part of puberty. In time, you will gain more control of your body and its responses.

Another change that God created for your developing body is the production of a fluid called semen. Semen helps transport sperm from your testicles out of your body. Semen is produced and stored in your prostate gland, located below the bladder along the urinary tract. Semen is not urine from your bladder. Sometimes your body produces more semen than it needs and you will wake up to find that your penis has released a small amount of thick fluid into your underwear. This is called a nocturnal emission or wet dream. Nocturnal emissions are natural; all young men have them. Simply be responsible to clean anything that may have become soiled.

LOOK OUT! GRENADE!: Our enemy, who has been around a long time and is well entrenched, often openly attacks us. Other times, he mounts sneak attacks. Either way, he uses the things we see and hear to infiltrate our minds. This affects not only our waking thoughts, but our subconscious thoughts and dreams as well. Maybe you saw or heard something inappropriate. Perhaps you noticed it only briefly and were able to ignore it, but later your memory pulled it up to review. This is evidence of infiltration. Sometimes we recognize infiltration while we are awake and other times after we wake from a dream.

Inappropriate TV shows and movies can trigger sexual thoughts or feelings. They are grenades that trigger hormone

> **"When I see something inappropriate, I turn off the television – or look the other way – or leave – depending on the circumstances."**
> **~JH**

activity in your body, producing excess semen and leading to more frequent nocturnal emissions. Don't allow inappropriate images to fester inside your heart and mind. Rather, confess your struggle to your Base of Operations (God and Dad). Confession often is all that is needed to make the temptation die away.

Take stock. Evaluate your friends. Are they talking about inappropriate things? Are you watching things that are eroding your moral strength? It's vitally important to protect your spiritual health and prevent the enemy from infiltrating your mind. Make sure to protect your mind, even as you sleep. As you go to bed, think wholesome thoughts and pray for the protection of your mind as you sleep. Ask the Lord to set a hedge around your mind to keep the enemy from planting anything unwholesome.

If your heart is clean, don't feel guilty about a nocturnal emission. They can happen quite naturally and through no fault of your own. A natural nocturnal emission could be discouraging to someone who has decided to be sexually pure. In such cases don't let what is natural discourage you from your commitment to purity in thought and deed.

> **"When my friends and I see something we shouldn't, like in a movie, we all say to each other, 'time to tie your shoes' then we bend over to avoid the temptation."**
> **~TK**

LOOK OUT! GRENADE!: Another grenade may explode on your spiritual journey. When your penis becomes erect you may be tempted to touch yourself in an inappropriate way, causing an ejaculation (release of semen). God created certain feelings exclusively for a husband and his wife. Having them outside of marriage cheats you and your future wife. Faithfulness doesn't start just after you are married; it starts now. Save all of yourself for your wife. Others may say that touching yourself in this way (called self-stimulation or masturbation) is normal and boys should do it if they wish. However, Colossians 2:8 tells us to "See to it that no one takes you captive through hollow and deceptive philosophy, which depends on human tradition and the basic principles of this world rather than on Christ."

There are four main scriptural reasons why masturbation is wrong. First, people who do this feel guilty even if they've been told it is okay or normal. This is a clear indication that the Holy Spirit is saying it is morally wrong. "...their consciences also bearing witness, and their thoughts now accusing, now even defending them" (Romans 2:15). The Holy Spirit speaks to your conscience. Never try to prevent Him from talking to your spirit. The more you ignore the Holy Spirit, the harder it will be to hear Him—even when you really want to. Listen to that quiet voice inside directing you to flee youthful lusts.

Second, those who masturbate find it becomes a habit that is hard to break, even after marriage. This cheats your spouse and causes pain and guilt. It is truly a grenade to avoid. Anything that binds you to a destructive habit is not God's best. Habits that are addictive are bondage. Many men mistakenly think they will satisfy their sexual desires by masturbating only to find masturbation increases their sexual desire. Feeding a habit makes it grow in strength. Only starving it will kill it. "Jesus replied, 'I tell you the truth, everyone who sins is a slave to sin'" (John 8:34).

Third, masturbation is a selfish behavior. A person who does it is only thinking about himself and what he wants. God has called us to be selfless, not to seek our own pleasures. He has called us to lay down our lives and our selfish desires to serve Him and others. If you enter a marriage with selfish habits, you will harm your relationship with your wife. Marriage is about two people giving to one another, not taking. "Love...is not self-seeking" (1 Corinthians 13:4-5).

Fourth, masturbation leads to other sins. The cruel master of Lust is quick to set up camp in any heart where masturbation has been permitted. Other enemy agents will join him –

enemies such as deceit, guilt and deeper areas of lust and bondage. Close the door to all of them at the outset. Refuse to allow this grenade to blow up in your heart. This will save you from countless other attempts on your spiritual life. "Then, after desire has conceived, it gives birth to sin; and sin, when it is full-grown, gives birth to death. Don't be deceived, my dear brothers" (James 1:15-16).

COUNTERATTACK #1: Your best counterattack will always be the Word of God. Check out the chapter titled, "Battle Ground: The Enemy's Schemes" for Scriptures you can memorize or meditate on. The Word of God is your sword, slicing the power of the enemy's attack and affording you a quick get away.

"When I am tempted, I remember the verses I have learned to resist the temptations." ~JH

"For the word of God is living and active. Sharper than any double-edged sword, it penetrates even to dividing soul and spirit, joints and marrow; it judges the thoughts and attitudes of the heart." Hebrews 4:12

COUNTERATTACK #2: Your prayer life and relationship with God is a primary line of defense when the enemy throws a grenade in your path. In any military operation, the enemy will first try to destroy your lines of communication. If he can isolate you, he can keep you from calling for help or hearing vital encouragement and support. Your loving heavenly Father desires that you run to Him in battle. He knows you can't win on your own. He wants you to lean on Him.

"Trust in the Lord with all your heart and lean not on your own understanding; in all your ways acknowledge him, and he will make your paths straight." Proverbs 3:5-6

COUNTERATTACK #3: Tell your Dad about this attack.

Your dad is probably your greatest earthly ally in the war for your heart. God and Dad are your Base of Operations. Go to them when you are under attack or need a fresh supply of wisdom or a place to rest. Dad will encourage you and tell you what he has learned by fighting the same battle. It can be difficult to start this conversation, but just jump in and say, "Dad, I am struggling in my heart in the area of lust." Your dad wants to help you avoid tempting situations. He can help figure out where the grenades have come from. If your dad is not able or available to discuss these critical issues, be bold and search out a True Man in your church or school who has sons with godly character. Ask him if he will advise you and become your ally in this mission. Your mom is also on your side. Share struggles with her so she can pray for you and encourage you.

"Listen, my sons, to a father's instruction; pay attention and gain understanding. I give you sound learning, so do not forsake my teaching." Proverbs 4:1-2

PLAN OF ATTACK: A True Man is master of his own body. Determine to develop moral character and not be captive to your developing body. Use the weapons listed above to mount a counterattack against Satan's offense. Counterattacking this grenade, called "Lust," can be trying, but it can be done.

TACTICAL REASONING: A True Man avoids as many grenades as possible by knowing his own weaknesses and avoiding danger.

COURSE SELECTION: Choose between following the way of lust or following God's path to manhood.

"...a man is a slave to whatever has mastered him." 2 Peter 2:19

BATTLEGROUND: GATES TO YOUR CITY

Proverbs 25:28 says, "Like a city whose walls are broken down is a man who lacks self-control." If you were to picture yourself as a city with great walls of self-control, fortified with the Word of God and a moat of wisdom, where would your vulnerability be? The most vulnerable points in any walled city are its gates. If your gates allow in evil attackers, what good are your wonderful walls? Even if you had your gates shut tight, where do you think your enemy would attack first? Would he knock on your wall or go to the most susceptible place first: your gate?

Like a walled city, you too have gates: your ears and eyes. No matter how strong your self-control, if you choose to allow the enemy in through what you hear or see, he will take over and destroy you.

"Your outer defense perimeters- protecting your eyes and your mind- will defend against sexual impurities. Your inner defense perimeter is your HEART. Protect it and keep it pure."
~OP

The second major change during this time is that your ears, and especially your eyes, become more aware of things you never noticed before. Now this doesn't mean you suddenly develop x-ray vision and supersonic hearing. But now your ears may perk up when someone mentions a certain girl's name. A few years ago, cars were just cars. But now you can tell the difference between different engines' sounds or determine the make of a car by the shape of its hood or the curve of its fender. Your taste for what kind of car you like is developing and so is your appreciation for the appearance of a young lady. The girls you once ignored or avoided are actually not that bad, maybe even attractive. Your eyes have opened.

EYES

An old proverb says, "The eyes are the windows to the soul" which means you can often tell what's on a person's heart, whether they are happy or sad, by what you "see" in their eyes. The eyes are also portals to the soul. Whatever you see can affect your heart. It is important that you guard your heart by guarding your eyes.

"I ponder my feet. This may be walking down the street or other places where there is visual info I don't want in my mind." ~DG

"I consciously focus my eyes on the eyes or faces of other people in a crowd to avoid seeing what I don't want see" ~TL

"Above all else, guard your heart, for it is the wellspring of life...Let your eyes look straight ahead, fix your gaze directly before you."
Proverbs 4:23, 25

LOOK OUT! GRENADE!:

In our world today, many dangers come through our eyes. Inappropriate images are all around you. Satan uses them to catch your eyes and lure you into deeper danger. The enemy twists things intended as good—tools like the Internet, billboards and television—

"The images that are recorded on our minds will be used by the enemy of our soul to torment us eventually interfering with our relationship with God and the scriptural values we want to live by." ~JD

and uses them to attack the purity of men. Satan uses lust to attack you. Provocatively dressed or naked images in books, magazines, TV or movies are intended to entice you sexually. This is called pornography. Pornography is not just a grenade, it is an RPG —a rocket propelled grenade! Satan doesn't use it just to injure you or destroy you slowly; he seeks to annihilate you. Looking at pornography is like going into enemy occupied territory. You cannot expect to go there and not suffer injury. No matter how strong you think you are, when you are on the enemy's turf, he will strike to kill.

"We have a TV guardian and internet / email filters for the computers."
~DJ

You know you should avoid some places and images. Pornography is way out of bounds for what is right. But there will be times when the enemy throws a grenade where you least expect it. You know not to turn on certain TV shows or stations, but the enemy may launch a grenade at school, the mall, or even church! Something may appear that you weren't looking for and didn't expect.

Just because the enemy throws a grenade your way doesn't mean you have to let it explode in your face! You can avoid the explosion. But you must be prepared and have a battle strategy. You must act quickly! If you stay too close, it will explode and injure you. The enemy will ambush anyone who is standing still too long in his territory. When a good friend starts telling an inappropriate story, what are you going to do? When you're innocently walking in the mall and an image you never intended to see suddenly hooks you, what plan do you have to keep the explosion of lust from reaching your heart? A True Man will take action to toss the grenade away.

We have control of our eyes. We can close our eyes as soon as we question what we are looking at."
~JD

COUNTERATTACK: First, remember it is not your fault when the enemy throws grenades at you. He does this to every man. As long as you are not searching for grenades, you don't have to feel guilty when Satan throws one your way. When you are caught off guard, you are not sinning; when you know where the grenades are and don't avoid them—that is sin. When you linger near a grenade, you foolishly choose to sin. This is a heart issue. Be honest with yourself and make every effort to navigate around grenades. Some guys lie to themselves, saying things like, "I can handle it. It doesn't affect me. I can look at this for a minute, it won't hurt me." The enemy uses these lies to appeal to your pride and arrogance and reel you in toward a grenade. Pride is a weakness. Don't be fooled into thinking that you are invincible.

"The major technique which I use when seeing (something inappropriate) that catches your attention is to simply have a long blink and turn your head. I find that this works for me – it gives my heart a chance to tell my head to not look."
~GB

Once a grenade is thrown in your path, what do you do? Run for cover! Make your eyes run away from what they have seen. Send them off like arrows in another direction. Focus on something else. You are in control of your eyes. If you look back at something impure or linger on something inappropriate, your look has become lust. Choose today to make a covenant with your eyes to keep them pure.

"You have heard that it was said, 'Do not commit adultery.' But I tell you that anyone who looks at a woman lustfully has already committed adultery with her in his heart."
Matthew 5:27-28

"I made a covenant with my eyes not to look lustfully at a girl."
Job 31:1

EARS

Your ears are another vulnerable gate to your city. Your ears are your own and you alone are responsible for what goes into them. What you hear has the power to stick in your mind and influence your heart and beliefs. If you hear things that are inappropriate and contrary to the Word of God, weed them out.

LOOK OUT! GRENADE!: Grenades that attack your ears come in several forms. Music, television, movies, friends or acquaintances that speak disrespectfully of women can all become grenades. You may think you are not doing anything wrong because you do not tell dirty jokes, but listening to them is just as bad. If someone around you is tossing grenades into your ears, you have the right and responsibility to protect your heart by shutting that person down. You don't want to hurt your friend's feelings, but you should never be willing to sacrifice your heart for entertainment or a friendship.

It can be tempting to participate in discussions about your changing body or share sexual information with other young men. Whenever you have personal questions, take them to your parents, not your friends. Your peers can give you bad information. They can also hurt you by sharing information you aren't ready for. If someone tries to talk to you about personal matters, tell him to speak to his dad. If he doesn't want to talk to his own father, ask him if he would talk to your father. It is not your job to discuss private matters with anyone but your parents.

COUNTERATTACK: Shut down friends who are out of control by saying things like, "I'm sorry, but I really don't want to hear that" or "Hey, that's not cool." If they persist, be strong enough to leave. Some boys may accuse you of not being a real man because you don't listen to their stories, jokes or advice, but remember that a True Man is committed to keep his own way pure and is not driven by the lusts of flesh or the opinions of others. His Lord defines his way. Men are called to be protectors of women. One way you can protect women is by keeping your thoughts about them pure and encouraging those around you to do the same.

"Nor should there be obscenity, foolish talk or coarse joking, which are out of place, but rather thanksgiving." Ephesians 5:4

"Flee the evil desires of youth, and pursue righteousness, faith, love and peace, along with those who call on the Lord out of a pure heart." 2 Timothy 2:22

PROTECTING THE GATES TO YOUR CITY

PLAN OF ATTACK: When your eyes and ears are under attack, act quickly to shut the gates and destroy the invader.

TACTICAL REASONING: A wise man avoids hostile territory and guards his eyes and ears at all times, even when he thinks the enemy is nowhere in sight.

COURSE SELECTION: Choose to guard your heart by watching what you allow in your gates.

"I will be careful to lead a blameless life – when will you come to me? I will walk in my house with blameless heart. I will set before my eyes no vile thing." Psalm 101:2-3

"When I'm tempted to look at something I shouldn't, I 'bounce' my eyes to something else and continue on my way." ~TK

"Turn my eyes away from worthless things." Psalm 119:37

BATTLEGROUND: THE ENEMY'S SCHEMES

"Put on the full armor of God so that you can take your stand against the devil's schemes." Ephesians 6:11

"Be self-controlled and alert. Your enemy the devil prowls around like a roaring lion looking for someone to devour." 1 Peter 5:8

"...that they will come to their senses and escape from the trap of the devil, who has taken them captive to do his will." 2 Timothy 2:26

In Genesis 1:28, God tells us that when He first created man He told him to subdue and rule over the earth, not in a heavy-handed way, but as a prince cares for those responsibilities the King places in his charge. Before any man can rightly rule over anything in creation he must rule over himself. You must learn to have ***self***-control before you are given the control of anything else.

"Don't wait for a temptation to come. Prepare in advance and decide what you will do. Think through the consequences." ~DH

The enemy doesn't want you to grow in self-control. Self-control renders his attacks on you ineffective. He wants you to be his prey. It is important that you are aware of his schemes and tactics so you can withstand his attacks. We've already explored many of Satan's schemes through the different grenades he throws, but now let's explore some "strategic vulnerabilities" Satan tries to exploit. By doing this, you will be wise to his methods and not fall into his traps. Let's also learn about the weapons God has given to us to fight Satan's schemes.

STRATEGIC VULNERABILITY: YOUR MIND

Satan primarily attacks your mind. The importance of what you think about cannot be overstated. The enemy will use emotions of self-pity, anger, guilt, loneliness or pride to encourage thoughts such as, "Nothing I do matters," "My feelings are natural so why fight it?" "I can't help it," "It's my body," or "No one will know."

These are common phrases the enemy uses to lure us into compromise. When you hear yourself thinking thoughts like these, realize that the enemy is at work! He is throwing another grenade into your thought life. This is harassing fire intended to lower your morale and make you surrender. It's time for a counterattack. Fight back! Don't listen! Fight the enemy's thoughts with God's thoughts.

> **"When I'm tempted to think about something I shouldn't, I repeat in my head, 'Whatever is pure, whatever is right, whatever is of good report, dwell on such things.'"**
> **~TK**

Scriptures are a power-packed way to fight back. Commit some to memory so they are available to you when you need them no matter where you are. By using Scripture, you are exploiting the enemy's weakness. God's Word has the final say. Here are some Scriptures that can help you wage an effective counterattack when you are in a battle:

VERSES TO HELP YOU IN YOUR THOUGHT LIFE:

"We demolish arguments and every pretension that sets itself

up against the knowledge of God, and we take captive every thought to make it obedient to Christ." 2 Corinthians 10:5

From 2 Corinthians 10:5 ('...we take captive every thought to make it obedient to Christ') I pretend there is a trap in my mind. When a bad thought enters my mind, I snap the trap on the bad thought and destroy it."
~DJ

"Above all else, guard your heart, for it is the wellspring of life." Proverbs 4:23

"Finally, brothers, whatever is true, whatever is noble, whatever is right, whatever is pure, whatever is lovely, whatever is admirable – if anything is excellent or praiseworthy – think about such things." Philippians 4:8

"Therefore, I urge you, brothers, in view of God's mercy, to offer your bodies as living sacrifices, holy and pleasing to God – this is your spiritual act of worship. Do not conform any longer to the pattern of this world, but be transformed by the renewing of your mind. Then you will be able to test and approve what God's will is – his good, pleasing and perfect will." Romans 12:1-2

VERSES TO HELP YOU CONTROL YOUR EYES:

"I will be careful to lead a blameless life – when will you come to me? I will walk in my house with blameless heart. I will set before my eyes no vile thing." Psalm 101:2-3

"I made a covenant with my eyes not to look lustfully at a girl." Job 31:1

"It will be useful to memorize several verses of scripture about purity, because they will work to transform and wash your mind. But in this day-to-day fight you need one simple quick attack verse. I suggest Job 31:1 'I made a covenant with my eyes.'"
~AP

"You have heard that it was said, 'Do not commit adultery.' But I tell you that anyone who looks at a woman lustfully has already committed adultery with her in his heart." Matthew 5:27-28

"With eyes full of adultery, they never stop sinning; they seduce the unstable; they are experts in greed – an accursed brood! They have left the straight way." 2 Peter 2:14-15

"For everything in the world – the cravings of sinful man, the lust of his eyes and the boasting of what he has and does – comes not from the Father but from the world. The world and its desires pass away, but the man who does the will of God lives forever." 1 John 2:16-17

"Do not lust in your heart after her beauty or let her captivate you with her eyes." Proverbs 6:25

VERSES TO HELP YOU WITH SELF CONTROL:

"Similarly, encourage the young men to be self-controlled." Titus 2:6

"...a man is a slave to whatever has mastered him." 2 Peter 2:19

"It is God's will that you should be sanctified: that you should avoid sexual immorality; that each of you should learn to control his own body in a way that is holy and honorable, not in passionate lust like the heathen, who do not know God." 1 Thessalonians 4:3-5

"The moment that you think to yourself that I shouldn't think of 'x,' is the moment you are thinking about it, so don't think about not doing it, know what you should do and act accordingly."
~TK

"Flee the evil desires of youth, and pursue righteousness, faith, love and peace, along with those who call on the Lord out of a pure heart." 2 Timothy 2:22

"...my son, I give you this instruction in keeping with the prophecies once made about you, so that by following them you may fight the good fight, holding on to faith and a good conscience. Some have rejected these and so have shipwrecked their faith." 1 Timothy 1:18-19

VERSES ON GODLY LIVING:

"...I want you to be wise about what is good, and innocent about what is evil." Romans 16:19

"I find that the busier I am, the less time I have to be tempted." ~TK

"Fear God and keep his commandments, for this is the whole duty of man. For God will bring every deed into judgment, including every hidden thing, whether it is good or evil." Ecclesiastes 12:13-14

"But set an example for the believers in speech, in life, in love, in faith and in purity." 1 Timothy 4:12

"Treat...older women as mothers, and younger women as sisters, with absolute purity." 1 Timothy 5:1-2

"How can a young man keep his way pure? By living according to your word. I seek you with all my heart; do not let me stray from your commands. I have hidden your word in my heart that I might not sin against you." Psalm 119:9-11

"If you are convicted that some thing is right before God, you will do it and not care what others think and do. Don't hang out with those who have a bad influence on you." ~JH

"For we are God's workmanship, created in Christ Jesus to do good works, which God prepared in advance for us to do." Ephesians 2:10

VERSES ON SEXUAL IMMORALITY:

"But among you there must not be even a hint of sexual immorality, or of any kind of impurity, or of greed, because these are improper for God's holy people." Ephesians 5:3

"You can win this battle by training your eyes to bounce away from sights of pretty women and sensual images."
~UM

"For God did not call us to be impure, but to live a holy life." 1 Thessalonians 4:7

"The body is not meant for sexual immorality, but for the Lord, and the Lord for the body." 1 Corinthians 6:13

"Flee from sexual immorality. All other sins a man commits are outside his body, but he who sins sexually sins against his own body. Do you not know that your body is a temple of the Holy Spirit, who is in you, whom you have received from God? You are not your own; you were bought at a price. Therefore honor God with your body." 1 Corinthians 6:18-20

"But a man who commits adultery lacks judgment; whoever does so destroys himself." Proverbs 6:32

"I saw among the simple, I noticed among the young men, a youth who lacked judgment. He was going down the street near her corner, walking along in the direction of her house...With persuasive words she led him astray; she seduced him with her smooth talk. All at once he followed her like an ox going to the slaughter, like a deer stepping into a noose till an arrow pierces his liver, like a bird darting into a snare, little knowing it will cost him his life. Now then, my sons, listen to me; pay attention to what I say. Do not let your heart turn to her ways or stray into her paths. Many are the victims she has brought down; her slain are a mighty throng. Her house is a highway to the grave, leading down to the chambers of death." Proverbs 7:7-8, 21-27 (Notice

how the young man's lack of judgment starts with where he is headed and how his heart has led him there.)

SATAN'S SCHEME: Deception. The enemy will fight for control of your mind. If he can rule your thoughts, he can rule all of you.

GOD'S WEAPON: The Word of God is a sword you must learn to wield. Your skill with this weapon will decide your fate.

"The weapons we fight with are not the weapons of the world. On the contrary, they have divine power to demolish strongholds." 2 Corinthians 10:4

STRATEGIC VULNERABILITY: ISOLATION

"No temptation has seized you except what is common to man."1 Corinthians 10:13

Notice this verse says that the temptation you will experience is "common to man." You are not in this battle alone. The more like-minded people you gather around you to hold you accountable, the better off you'll be. All soldiers know you don't go off on a mission alone. If you take fellow soldiers along, you can protect each other and come out alive.

"When one surrounds himself with other young men, with mentors, and engages with his father who is committed to encouraging rather than condemning, then one has an invaluable support group that offers encouragement and love and motivation to live in purity. As he grows then God's love and faithfulness and forgiveness begins to replace the external incentives that have given him motivation."
~PC

To keep you isolated, the enemy may try

to make you feel prideful. Often young men have a false sense that they know everything. They feel they are independent and don't need to learn from others. This is a scheme of the enemy. He knows that your strength will increase as you are teachable.

It may sound strange, because most young people think that maturity means knowing everything and being able to do your own thing. But the more teachable and humble you are, the more mature you will be. Choose relationships that keep you accountable to God, then you will become a mature, strong True Man.

"For waging war you need guidance, and for victory many advisers." Proverbs 24:6

"Two are better than one, because they have a good return for their work: If one falls down, his friend can help him up. But pity the man who falls and has no one to help him up!" Ecclesiastes 4:9-10

SATAN'S SCHEME: Isolate. The enemy knows that if he can isolate you, he can get you to believe lies and make you think you can get away with sin. Then he will beat you up with condemnation, guilt and fear.

GOD'S WEAPON: Relationship. Choose fellow soldiers who will watch your back. Listen to the Lord's leading so that you can choose wisely. Talk openly with your dad about struggles or concerns. You may also find a godly friend or mentor that can be a fellow soldier.

"Instead, speaking the truth in love, we will in all things grow up into him who is the Head, that is, Christ. From him the whole body, joined and held together by every supporting ligament, grows and builds itself up in love, as each part does its work." Ephesians 4:15-16

STRATEGIC VULNERABILITY: BOREDOM

One of the enemy's classic schemes is to exploit the dangerous combination of boredom and excess energy. In the old days people used to say, "Idleness is the devil's workshop" which means that when you're bored, the enemy will suggest all kinds of wrong things you can do.

> **"I have heard and seen that boys who are active in sports don't have a lot of free time on their hands to dwell on things that they shouldn't. I think being involved in any activity, such as music performance where a great deal of practice is required, is also helpful."**
> **~DJ**

Have a plan for when you find yourself getting bored and tempted. Find an activity that you enjoy, preferably something that engages your mind and your body. Sports are a great outlet. If you aren't into organized sports, you can go for a run, ride a bike, or just walk outside. Meditating on wholesome things while you do these is a must. Listen to Christian music, pray, or recite your favorite Scriptures. Divert your mind from temptation and focus on "whatever is true, whatever is noble, whatever is right, whatever is pure, whatever is lovely, whatever is admirable…" (Philippians 4:8).

The enemy can also attack you if you spend too much time alone. If you are tempted while you are alone, choose to be with people, keep your bedroom door open, or talk to a friend via a phone or computer. The enemy likes to make our minds get stuck on impure things so choose to divert your mind and avoid the grenades. Remove opportunities to do wrong.

God created your body as His temple so the enemy would like nothing more than to highjack your body and use it for his temple. Your body is fearfully and wonderfully made. Honoring God with your body is a way of giving Him thanks for His creation. We are created by God and for God.

SATAN'S SCHEME: Idleness. Satan finds it much easier to tempt us when we are bored and have too much time on our hands.

GOD'S WEAPON: Keep yourself occupied. Focus your mind on your body's purpose and keep yourself busy with fun and productive things.

"Do you not know that your body is a temple of the Holy Spirit, who is in you, whom you have received from God? You are not your own; you were bought at a price. Therefore honor God with your body." 1 Corinthians 6:19-20

STRATEGIC VULNERABILITY: MISCALCULATION OF PURITY

It is tempting to believe that because you haven't had sex, you are pure. Purity is much more than what you do with your body. True purity goes much deeper — it goes to your heart. Jesus continually tells us that God is concerned with your heart. He says that doing all the right things doesn't make you clean. God knows that if you keep your heart pure, the rest of you will be pure as well. Jesus told those who were trying to do the bare minimum to achieve purity, "First clean the inside of the cup and dish, and then the outside also will be clean" (Matthew 23:26). If you work to keep your heart pure, your actions will be pure as well.

"In the heat of sexual temptation, what will it mean to not offer your body to sin, as Paul says? Ask yourself, what will offering myself to God require of me?" ~DR

Naturally, you want to save all of yourself for your future wife – not just making love, but your first kiss and maybe even holding hands. Saving physical acts of intimacy for your wife are important, but what about your heart? If you give your heart away to a girl you may never marry or if you entertain thoughts and feelings that should be saved for your future wife, you are giving pieces of yourself away. You are stealing from your future wife what rightfully belongs to her and placing it into the hands of those who have no right to you.

What you do with your body is important—it is God's temple—but never neglect your heart. All the issues of life flow out of it. To be truly pure, your heart must be pure.

SATAN'S SCHEME: Compromise. If the enemy can get you on the slippery slope of compromise, he can cause impurity to latch onto your heart.

GOD'S WEAPON: Guard your heart as if your life depended on it. Recognize that true purity needs to be more than what you do or don't do. It needs to be who you are.

"Flee the evil desires of youth, and pursue righteousness, faith, love and peace, along with those who call on the Lord out of a pure heart." 2 Timothy 2:22

"Above all else, guard your heart, for it is the wellspring of life." Proverbs 4:23

STRATEGIC VULNERABILITY: FIGHTING DIRTY

One tactic the enemy may use: fighting dirty. While you are working to maintain a pure heart, Satan may tempt you to fight his way. He may try to get you to compromise your battle tactics. He may tell you to fight against lust by using pride. He may deceive you into thinking you are too good to fall into a particular sin. Others may struggle with it, but you don't. But we know pride comes before a fall.

He may tell you that you must fight lust in order to please

other people. But this is not why we fight lust. We fight lust because it is of Satan and sinful. The shame Satan brings will prevent you from talking to someone about your struggle with lust. This will only make life harder. Fear of rejection will make you afraid to share with your dad or pastor. Satan knows that sharing a burden makes it lighter and it makes you less vulnerable to attacks.

Fighting against one vice (weakness) by using another vice is fighting on Satan's terms. 2 Corinthians 10:4 reminds us that "the weapons we fight with are not the weapons of the world. On the contrary, they have divine power to demolish strongholds." Don't use a vice to conquer or control another vice. That may help you suppress a bad behavior for a time, but the behavior doesn't really go away and now your sin has multiplied. You must use the weapons the Lord gives you—the Word of God and your relationship with Him.

"When a train of thought gets stuck in my mind that I don't want there, I sing a love song to my God that He gave me years ago as my way of escape."
~TL

Use the virtue that is the opposite of what you are trying to conquer. When you are fighting lust, fight with love—love for God and His divine ways and love for your future spouse. When you are fighting pride, fight with humility. Don't think you know everything. Ask for help and offer help to others. When you fear people's opinions, fight back by tightening your belt of truth and being brave enough to talk to someone about what you're feeling. When you are tempted to believe that what you do doesn't matter, remember that out there somewhere is the perfect wife for you who wants very much for you to hold onto what is pure and right.

SATAN'S SCHEME: Multiply sin by fighting a vice with another vice.

GOD'S WEAPON: Fight with God's weapons. Use the fruit of the Spirit as your arsenal.

"Some trust in chariots and some in horses, but we trust in the name of the Lord our God." Psalm 20:7

"But the fruit of the Spirit is love, joy, peace, patience, kindness, goodness, faithfulness, gentleness and self-control. Against such things there is no law." Galatians 5:22-23

STRATEGIC VULNERABILITY: THE IDENTITY ATTACK

A common attack Satan is using in this age is to get young men to question whether they are homosexual (attracted to a person of the same gender). Many young men, even Christian young men, are being attacked with a deadly weapon. This weapon is like an arrow. The first time it hits its victim, it is extremely painful and if the Physician (Jesus) does not remove it, Satan will repeatedly press the arrow deeper, closer and closer to the heart. With every blow, the victim fears that perhaps he deserves it; he wonders if he is a homosexual.

Satan's arrows can come in a variety of forms and leave a variety of wounds. The arrow may come in the form of being sexually molested (inappropriately touched). He may use the arrow of being teased about physical development. He may exploit the painful arrow of a sexual experience with a boy or man. These arrows can cause a young man to lose sight of God's truth that he was created to be attracted to girls. We must submit our thoughts and experiences to God and choose to believe what God says about us. Sins committed against you do not define you, God defines you. If an arrow of abuse has hit you, it isn't your fault and there is no shame in bringing that injury to your parent's attention. Don't let an injury go without attention. It can become infected if it doesn't get the proper care.

Secular culture is working to shift public opinion to accept homosexual behavior as normal and acceptable. People are focusing intently on homosexuality: it is very much on everybody's mind. As a result of this attention, young men are falsely being led to believe that they too may be homosexual. Some individuals have convinced the world that "some people are just born that way." We know differently. God created men to behave as men and women to behave as women. He is a loving Father who designed us to live an abundant life. He commands that people not practice homosexuality. He would never make a command impossible to obey by creating people who are homosexuals. Most men who practice homosexuality have been cruelly abused. That was their arrow. Once the enemy had the arrow in them, he repeatedly sabotaged them with hateful comments and repeated abuse in order to convince them of his lie.

If you feel that you have been hit with the enemy's arrow, it's not too late. Begin talking to your parents and seek Christian counseling from someone who is experienced in removing this type of arrow. Above all, never believe the enemy's lie about you. Know that just as your Father in heaven has a wonderful plan for you, so the enemy of your soul has a plan: to destroy you. The arrows that have pierced you are not your fault. Satan knows that God's plans are good for you and he will try whatever he can to sabotage them. Don't let him have his way. Don't let him steal God's plan!

SATAN'S SCHEME: Attack your manhood. Cause you to doubt who you are and your intended purpose. Confirm the doubt often.

GOD'S WEAPON: Fight with the truth of God's Word! Know and confess that God created you in His image. Get help from someone who can speak God's truth over your life.

"Do not lie with a man as one lies with a woman; that is detestable." Leviticus 18:22

BATTLEGROUND: PROTECTING GIRLS, YOUNG WOMEN AND MOTHERS

Women are wonderful creations of God. They are God's final exclamation point on all of creation, His last piece of handiwork before He declared that, "it was very good" (Genesis 1:31). This book teaches young men to exercise caution toward women and treat them with respect. That is not because women are dangerous instruments of the enemy who want to lure you away from God. The truth is that because women are so precious, so very special, the enemy tries to misuse them. Satan is always trying to steal what God made beautiful and make it ugly.

Satan hates women. He knew that a woman would one day cooperate with God to produce One Who would crush him. Mary gave birth to Jesus, Who destroyed the works of Satan for all time. In Genesis 3:15, God tells Satan, "I will put enmity between you and the woman, and between your offspring and hers; he will crush your head, and you will strike his heel."

"Treat girls with great respect from an early age and become their protectors." ~SH

Because of his hatred for women, the enemy will attempt

to use you in his battle against them. God designed you to protect women; Satan will try to turn you into a predator. God designed you to provide for your future wife; Satan will try to make you a taker of women. He would like to take your love and care and turn it into lust.

Look at the life of Solomon. He was a young man who had everything going for him. He was king over the entire nation of Israel. God had given him wisdom to rule and through this wisdom he gained great respect and wealth. But lurking inside Solomon was a desire that no woman could fulfill. Solomon's desire for women consumed his life and his relationship with God. He turned his back on God and all he knew to be right in order to please and be pleased by the women in his life. He became a lustful taker instead of a loving giver.

Solomon made two common mistakes. First, he sought fulfillment in women instead of in God. Second, he thought he could compromise in the area of lust and still maintain a healthy relationship with God. His progressive compromises led him away from God and the wisdom God had given him. Because he allowed lust to rule him, he became what he dreaded: a fool. Solomon made women his god. He stopped worshipping the Creator and worshipped the creation.

SO HOW IS A YOUNG MAN TO TREAT WOMEN?

You don't have to make Solomon's mistake. You can learn the proper way to treat women. In 1 Timothy 5:2 Paul tells the young man, Timothy, that he should treat older women as if they were his mother and young women as if they were his sisters. Now, if you tease or pick on your sisters, this is not what Paul is telling Timothy to do! He is telling him that his thoughts and actions toward women should be pure. He should protect their honor. He should ensure that their virtue and purity is always preserved.

Some girls do not choose to protect their own purity and virtue, but even with them, you should always be a young man

"Bounce your eyes when they fall on inappropriately dressed women – bounce your eyes and look into their eyes steadily for a conversation"
~JB

with whom they are safe. Some girls may dress immodestly, but it should be known that you will choose to exercise self-control by keeping your eyes on their faces and not their bodies. You will need to limit the amount of time you spend around girls who choose not to protect themselves. This will help you to "abstain from all appearance of evil" (1 Thessalonians 5:22 KJV) and keep you from stumbling. When you are around them, you will need to put up extra guards at your eye gate.

Part of treating girls with respect means being a gentleman. Open doors for girls, give them your seat if there are none to be had, let them enter a room first, and quiet inappropriate talk around them. These are all ways to be a gentleman and fulfill God's calling as a protector. It is part of what separates boys from men.

Surprisingly, some girls have been taught that they should not allow young men to be gentlemanly toward them. They are taught that men who do so think they are weak or incapable. The truth is, women are capable, so capable they shouldn't have to prove it by doing everything themselves. If a young woman chides you for behaving gentlemanly, tell her that you are who you are: a gentleman. Don't change your good behavior to conform to those who don't understand your role as a True Man.

As you grow from a boy to a young man, you move from your mother's care to caring for yourself and others. You may care for others because they need the help, but sometimes you may choose to honor and bless them by placing their needs above yours. This is how you should treat Mom, your sisters, and the girls at school or church.

In general, girls should not be treated like the guys you hang out with, your brothers, or your dad. Instead of racing to the door and then holding it closed, you should open the door for your sisters, girls at school, and women at church or the mall.

Not every girl will want the door opened for her, but look for chances to assist someone simply to bless her.

As young men you need to ensure the safety of those around you. This is your responsibility. Walk on the street side of the sidewalk, closest to the road, when a girl is with you. Walk her to her car in the parking lot, ensuring she is not alone. Stand in defense of anyone being picked on or harassed. Your goal is to become an observant, caring man who sees what needs to be done and acts on it. God has given you strength and a warrior nature for a reason and you should use it to protect and help those around you.

Here are examples of how a True Man should treat women.

- Opening doors (car, house, school, etc.)
- Carrying heavy objects (books, groceries, etc.)
- Standing up against bullies
- Letting them order first at a restaurant
- Letting them go before you in a line at the store, theater, or restaurant
- Helping with their chair at a restaurant
- Removing your hat at the table
- Taking the street side of the sidewalk; putting yourself between the noise, the cars, and them
- No tackling, chasing, tickling, or general roughhousing at the wrong time or too roughly
- No interrupting them when they are talking
- Exercising consideration at mealtime by using manners

WHAT IS GOING ON WITH THOSE GIRLS ANYWAY?

You may have noticed that the girls around you are growing up too. They are changing inside and out, just like you. Most of these changes enable girls to one day marry and have children. One is the beginning of menstruation, or "periods." This is a monthly occurrence for women who are not pregnant. When a woman's body recognizes that she is not pregnant, the fluid that has built up inside of her womb in order to protect a baby is flushed out. Women use feminine products like pads or tampons to capture this fluid.

If you have more questions, ask your mom or dad, but because this is a private matter, it is not something you should discuss with girls around you or your peers. Preserve girls' privacy and dignity by treating them with respect. Girls appreciate your sensitivity regarding their changes, just as you do. You would not want your personal information discussed in public. Neither do they.

How you treat and think about young women says a lot about who you are as a man. If it is difficult to treat or think about girls as you should, restrict yourself from being around them. If something is causing you to stumble, cut it out of your life. When your self-control is more developed, you can bring girls back into your life as sisters.

Women are more precious than gems, yet some men treat them like dirt. In response, some women accept the lie that they are dirt. Dirt is not worth protecting, it is common and has no value. But no matter how many men and women believe the lie, it will never be true. Women are gems. How will you treat the gems in your life? Will you protect them? Keep them pure and radiant; give them a place of honor.

"A wife of noble character who can find? She is worth far more than rubies." Proverbs 31:10

WAITING FOR THE RIGHT ONE

In our society, we are not content or accustomed to waiting for things. We want everything now. The same can be true of relationships. It can be difficult to wait until the proper time to have a relationship with a girl. Your desire for a wife is God-ordained. However, just because it is from God doesn't mean it is for right now. Just as you must wait for things like dinner and

Christmas, you must wait for God to guide you into a relationship with your future wife.

The key is to make your waiting time productive. When we wait impatiently or discontentedly, we miss so much. We miss the joys of everyday life. We miss opportunities to answer God's call in ways that we can only do while single. What does God have for you in this time of waiting? Focus on God and make your relationship with Him your top priority and He will give you all you need. Keep in mind that the way a young man treats his mom is often the way he will treat his wife! During this time of waiting, cultivate your skill of treating women well by practicing kindness, honor, and gentleness toward your mother. Ask yourself, "Is God satisfied with how I treat my mom?"

You have so many opportunities to look forward to before you add a young woman to your life. You need to finish your education and establish your career. You could go on mission trips to foreign countries or even in your neighborhood. "Delight yourself in the Lord and he will give you the desires of your heart" (Psalm 37:4).

This runs contrary to the way society thinks. You may find that friends and loved ones press you to become involved with girls before your time. Perhaps they tease you because you choose to wait for this special relationship. There may even be girls who call you or ask you to date them. Now is the time for you to be a good friend to them, not a romantic distraction. Keep in mind that you are responsible for your own heart. You are responsible to keep it pure and to save every bit of it for your wife. Don't give in to the pressure. Stand strong and you will be rewarded.

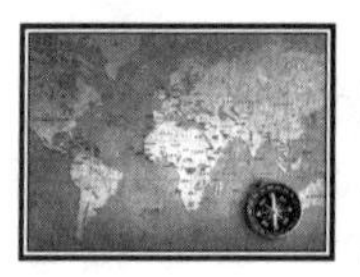

PLAN OF ATTACK: Treat the girls in your life appropriately: Treat the young girls and girls your age as sisters and the older women as you would want your mother and grandmothers to be treated.

TACTICAL REASONING: Treating girls as family members helps to keep your motives and actions pure. When you eventually marry the woman God brings to you, you will have kept your heart and body exclusively reserved for your wife. You will be able to give yourself freely.

COURSE SELECTION: Choose to be a protector of women, not a predator.

"Let us not become weary in doing good, for at the proper time we will reap a harvest if we do not give up." Galatians 6:9

BATTLEGROUND: GROWING INTO LEADERSHIP

Imagine that you live in the mid-1800's in America and grew up along the banks of the Ohio River. Every spring since you were about 10, you see wagon trains travel past your parent's home heading west to Wyoming, Montana or Colorado. Some wagons stop for the night at your house and the travelers talk to your parents about where they are going and what fortunes await them—new homesteads, ranches, farmlands or maybe furs from the beavers and foxes in the mountains of the western United States.

Now imagine that you are 31 years old and have been married for ten years and have several children. The Ohio valley has been experiencing a long drought and you must find a new place to settle and raise your family. You must move on or die. You remember those who have passed by your place and decide you are ready for that adventure.

As a young married man ready to leave the place of your youth, you realize that this is an important step. You will be on your own; you will have to lead your family across the wide expanse of empty prairie. You will have to provide food for yourself, your family and your horses. You will be responsible for their protection. You will have to select a destination and course of travel. You will have to ford rivers and climb mountains and endure the blazing heat of summer on the Great Plains to reach the place of your dreams. How will you do it?

As you make plans, you remember those who went before you. You realize that they left trails in the grass. They found places to ford the Mississippi and Missouri rivers. They discovered mountain passes. Some built towns along the way, laid up with provisions. Others even produced diaries, written records and maps providing direction and information.

You realize that while you must lead your family, you are not the first to do so. There are others to follow; you can look to those who have gone on before. Your confidence to face the wilderness grows. Your wife sees your diligent planning and steps up beside you. She trusts that you will bring her and her children safely across the grassy plains to a new home.

Life is not unlike this story. You will be living out an adventure. At some point you may have a wife and family to lead. Where will you get your direction? You will not be the first to travel the road you are on. Your earthly father has walked it before you. Our Abba Father, God, has also gone ahead. He knows every difficulty and trial. He has left a Guidebook and a Guide. The Bible is your Guidebook and the Holy Spirit is your Guide. When you look to them for direction and leadership, you will be able to lead as well. Whether leading your wife, family, or yourself, look to Jesus Christ to direct your steps.

Part of your mission to become a True Man is to become a leader. You will be the leader of a family. Your future wife and children will look to you for leadership in many areas. You can lead in your job, church, community, or in the government. But what about now—how can you prepare? As a young man there are opportunities to practice leadership. For example, you can lead a class discussion, a Bible Study, or a sports team. You also can exhibit good character to your friends and siblings.

But what is a leader? How does a leader know where to go? How does he learn how to get there? A good leader must follow a better leader. As Christians, Jesus Christ is our Leader. He sets the goals, the rules, and is the example. How do you become a leader? You follow Jesus' example.

JESUS WAS SUBMITTED TO HIS FATHER

Jesus spent approximately 30 years preparing to do what God called Him to do. During that time He grew up in His parents' home. He submitted to His earthly parents and to the Heavenly Father. As a young man learning carpentry in Joseph's home, He had to learn the same lessons that we all do. He had chores to do. He had to fix things He had broken. He had to get up in the morning after too little sleep and work to provide for the family. He was in training. He was God, but He submitted to His earthly father, Joseph, to learn a trade and help His parents. He served a man He Himself had created! He humbled Himself to practice the trade of carpentry under His earthly father's direction.

"Then he (Jesus) went down to Nazareth with them and was obedient to them (His parents)." Luke 2:51

Jesus was God, but He chose to empty Himself of all the power that made Him God and be obedient to the Father in order to be our example of how to live.

"Jesus gave them this answer: 'I tell you the truth, the Son can do nothing by himself; he can do only what he sees his Father doing, because whatever the Father does the Son also does.'" John 5:19

Leaders are not rebels, renegades, or lone rangers. They have authority because they submit to a higher authority. As you grow, others will recognize your leadership when it aligns with the authority your parents or teachers give you. Leaders are not independent people who do their own thing. Leaders do the right thing for others. If you step out from under God's authority, you move into a place of rebellion and sin. If you do not submit, your leadership will take others in the wrong direction.

There will be a proper time to step out from under your

parent's authority and be directly responsible to and under the authority of Christ. This is a natural process with its own timing. You can not make it happen. When Jesus began public ministry and left the home of His youth, He didn't leave in rebellion against His earthly parents. He continued to honor His parents even as He became independent from them. As you become an adult, your expression of submission to your parents shifts from obedience to honor. However, you will always submit to and obey God.

JESUS WAS A SERVANT

Jesus set the example of servant leadership. He was God yet He washed the dust and grime from His disciples' feet like a lowly household servant.

"After that, he poured water into a basin and began to wash his disciples' feet, drying them with the towel that was wrapped around him… 'Now that I, your Lord and Teacher, have washed your feet, you also should wash one another's feet.'"
John 13:5, 14

Jesus, as the God of the Universe, had every right to demand that His disciples serve Him, but His desire was to demonstrate the love of God and humble leadership.

There will be opportunities to lead as you grow through your teen years. Make sure you lead with a humble heart. Be willing to do the hard work, not just pass it onto others. Look around for people to help and bless. Find ways to promote growth in others and don't worry about recognition. Remember that leading is not always glamorous or glorious; it requires sacrifice and the desire to bless your family and friends.

JESUS USED HIS AUTHORITY TO STAND FOR WHAT IS RIGHT

Jesus was no wimp. As a carpenter, He was physically strong. As a leader, He was strong in His convictions and willing to act in bold and strong ways. He knew right and wrong and was willing to use His strength and authority to challenge those who did not follow the true heart of God, His Father. He was not concerned with popularity or the opinions of others; He was concerned only with the will of His Father.

"So he made a whip out of cords, and drove all from the temple area, both sheep and cattle; he scattered the coins of the money changers and overturned their tables. To those who sold doves he said, 'Get these out of here! How dare you turn my Father's house into a market!'" John 2:15

"He went into their synagogue, and a man with a shriveled hand was there. Looking for a reason to accuse Jesus, they asked him, 'Is it lawful to heal on the Sabbath?' He said to them, 'If any of you has a sheep and it falls into a pit on the Sabbath, will you not take hold of it and lift it out? How much more valuable is a man than a sheep! Therefore it is lawful to do good on the Sabbath.' Then he said to the man, 'Stretch out your hand.' So he stretched it out and it was completely restored, just as sound as the other." Matthew 12:9-13

Jesus was determined to do the right thing, no matter what. That was true when He purged impurity from the Holy Temple and when He challenged the false beliefs of the Pharisees. He was not hesitant to do what was required to make things right. He wanted to communicate how much God cared about people. Leadership isn't about shoving people around; it's about encouraging them forward. When people are being treated unjustly around you, are you willing to stand up for them as Jesus did? Are you willing to be a leader who sees wrong and acts to make it right? True Men don't complain about the world around them and do nothing. True Men are men of action.

JESUS WAS FAITHFUL

Jesus was a man Who could be trusted. If He said He would do something, you could count on Him to do it. Jesus kept His word even when it was extraordinarily difficult to do so. Jesus promised He would give His life so that we could be saved, but death on a cross and carrying everyone's sins is an unspeakably difficult task! What did Jesus do? He knew the people in Jerusalem would kill Him; nevertheless:

"As the time approached for him to be taken up to heaven, Jesus resolutely set out for Jerusalem." Luke 9:51

If you want to be a True Man you too must learn to be faithful. This means that when you make a promise or commitment, you follow through. Sometimes this won't be easy. You may be tempted to break a promise, but a True Man "keeps his oath even when it hurts" Psalm 15:4.

SOUNDING A CLEAR CALL

All who lead must have directions for where to go and how to get there. All good leaders follow Jesus the Commander. If you are a leader who does not obey the Lord or listen to His leading, you may fail to lead or lead others in the wrong direction.

In October 1854, the British were fighting the Crimean War with the Russian Empire. The British army commander, who was located on a ridge and could see more than the leaders in the valley, sent orders to the cavalry to stop the enemy from escaping with some weapons. However, the cavalry leader did not correctly hear the instructions and sent his men charging headlong into the strength of the Russian forces. The soldiers faithfully followed the orders and rode through the valley amid blazing gunfire. Many died or were injured—all because a leader did not correctly hear his commander's orders. (Alfred, Lord Tennyson memorialized this story in the poem "The Charge of the

Light Brigade.")

As a leader, it is critical that you have clear communication with your Commander, the Lord of Lords and King of Kings. Know your Commander, His Word, and His voice and you will avoid false commands. That way, people who depend on you won't get hurt or misled. This is a great responsibility. But God is faithful: when you spend time in prayer and Bible study, He will speak clearly. When you hear clearly, you will be able to sound the clear call and lead others victoriously through life's battles.

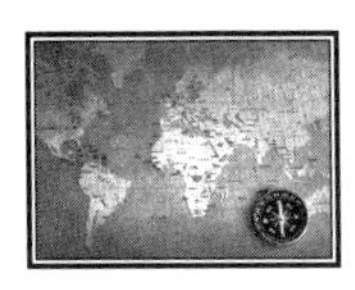

PLAN OF ATTACK: Be a leader who develops the character of Jesus.

TACTICAL REASONING: Leaders who are effective and respected are not pushy, arrogant or selfish; they submit to those in authority, serve others, and stand up for what's right.

COURSE SELECTION: As you become a leader, choose whom you will follow. You can lead in the manner of this world or you can lead in the manner exemplified by Jesus.

"Again, if the trumpet does not sound a clear call, who will get ready for battle?" 1 Corinthians 14:8

THE ANATOMY OF A TRUE MAN

The goal of this mission is to become a True Man. How are you doing? Have you chosen the right path? Are you sticking with it, growing ever stronger by exercising your spiritual muscles? As a young man, you have a choice. True Men make the right choice.

Psalm 15 describes a True Man. Paraphrased, Psalm 15 says, “Lord, whom do You really like to have around? What kind of person do You like to hang out with? I bet You like people who do their best to follow Your ways and are clean in Your eyes because Jesus removed all their sins. I bet You like people who are lovingly honest and don’t lie about others, who aren’t trying to hurt people in their actions or words. You like people who hate sin just like You do and respect those who respect and honor You. You like people who keep their word even if it causes them pain or inconvenience, who give freely without taking advantage of someone who is down and out. People like this never have any cause for fear.”

God has called all True Men to build the character traits of Psalm 15. You can do this through developing five primary relationships. These relationships are with God, the authorities in your life, your peers, those who are weaker than you, and your responsibilities. Take care of these five relationships and you will become a True Man.

YOUR RELATIONSHIP WITH GOD

> **"Studying the Bible, and not just reading it, has made me more serious and knowing what I believe, to know what is real and what is not."**
> **~DH**

The first and most important relationship is with God. He created you for relationship with Him. He desires to be your all and all, the One you go to all the time. He wants to be more than your Savior, but also that "friend who sticks closer than a brother" (Proverbs 18:24). He is not a distant God, but as close as your next breath. He longs for you to be His friend. "Come near to God and he will come near to you" (James 4:8).

YOUR RELATIONSHIP WITH AUTHORITY

The next relationship you must develop and maintain is with the authorities God has placed in your life. God has placed them over you and it is your duty to submit to them with a respectful attitude, even if you don't deem them worthy of respect. "Everyone must submit himself to the governing authorities, for there is no authority except that which God has established. All authorities that exist have been established by God. Consequently, he who rebels against the authority is rebelling against what God has instituted, and those who do so will bring judgment on themselves" (Romans 13:1-2).

The authorities in your life are your teachers, pastors and, most importantly, your parents. How you respond to these authorities speaks loudly about who you are. "Even a child is known by his actions, by whether his conduct is pure and right" (Proverbs 20:11). Being respectful when you disagree can be difficult, but as you exercise this spiritual muscle, God will honor you with strength and favor.

YOUR RELATIONSHIP WITH PEERS

Your relationship with peers also defines you as a man. Are you kind and encouraging to those around you? Do you build others up or tear them down? Are you a gentleman to the young women around you, treating them as sisters? Are you exhibiting the fruits of the Spirit when you are with other young men and young women? "... The fruit of the Spirit is love, joy, peace, patience, kindness, goodness, faithfulness, gentleness and self-control. Against such things there is no law" (Galatians 5:22).

YOUR RELATIONSHIP WITH THOSE WHO ARE WEAKER

"How far you go in life depends on your being tender with the young, compassionate with the aged, sympathetic with the striving and tolerant of the weak and strong. Because someday in your life you will have been all of these."
~George Washington Carver

The fourth relationship is with those who are weaker than you. Have you learned to be gentle when appropriate? Are you caring for younger siblings with tenderness? Are you respectfully helping the elderly? A True Man is never a bully. He recognizes that he has a duty, as a stronger member of our society, to protect those who are weaker. As Paul told the Thessalonians, "And we urge you, brothers, warn those who are idle, encourage the timid, help the weak, be patient with everyone" (1 Thessalonians 5:14).

YOUR RELATIONSHIP WITH RESPONSIBILITIES

The final relationship is with your stewardship responsibilities. God has given you abilities to nurture and tasks in your home. You are responsible to exercise care over your dominion. Practicing excellence in your schoolwork and taking care of God's world are part of your dominion. Your dominion—those things you are responsible for—will grow as you become more dependable. Don't neglect to take dominion where it is yours to take. "So if you have not been trustworthy in handling worldly wealth, who will trust you with true riches? And if you have not been trustworthy with someone else's property, who will give you property of your own?" (Luke 16:11-12).

Each relationship can stand alone, yet they are strongly dependent on one another. In the same way that your physical body is connected and you can't damage one part without affecting another, you cannot neglect one of these relationships and expect the others not to suffer. If you disrespect your parents, you rebel against God, for He established them as an authority over you. If you abuse your dominion by leaving messes everywhere, your peers may suffer. Most importantly, if you are not in a vibrant and growing relationship with God, every other area of your life will suffer. These five relationships reveal who you really are. What are they saying about you? Are you willing to work on them?

A True Man has a mind that is self-controlled and alert, hands that are ready to serve, feet that stand for what's right and flee from evil and, most importantly, a heart for God. Are you ready to develop the anatomy of a True Man?

PLAN OF ATTACK: Develop all the relationships in your life in a godly manner.

TACTICAL REASONING: Recognize that your relationships are a reflection of who you are.

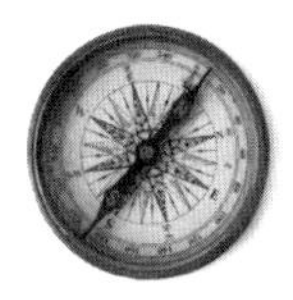

COURSE SELECTION: You must choose to live among those God has placed in your life with respect and care.

"Show proper respect to everyone: Love the brotherhood of believers, fear God, honor the king." 1Peter 2:17

MISSION BRIEFING

So now you have your mission, your goal. You've been through basic training and learned necessary maneuvers and tactics. You have been equipped to handle every challenge. Are you ready to face them? You are going to have great adventures and will win the war being waged against you. Our world needs young men like you. The church, the world, this nation, and your future family desperately need you to fulfill all God intended for you. When military soldiers go off to war they do not fight for their own lives, but for the lives of others. You are a soldier in the fight for our world. This fight is not just about you as an individual: you impact all those around you, which in turn impacts the world.

GO NOW AND FIGHT.

Other Books by this Author

The Miracle of Life

by Ami M. Loper and illustrated by Carol J. Loper

The birds and the bees, the classic method of relaying the miracle of life and reproduction to children is given a hand. This book provides parents the tool to facilitate this important conversation between parent and child from the youngest of ages. With informative text and illustrated with beautifully detailed flowers, this guide book will assist you and the children in your life as you together discover the "Miracle of Life."

The Miracle of Change – A Book for Young Ladies

by Ami M. Loper and illustrated by Carol J. Loper

Bring your daughter "back to the flower" at the age of transition to see the beauty in God's design and His plan for each blossom. This book is a delicate, yet honest look at the transformation that is coming your daughter's way. Help prepare your daughter for the miracle of change with this beautiful book that will celebrate her God - given femininity.